For

F.C.S.

The Child's First Books

A Critical Study of Pictures and Texts

by Donnarae MacCann
& Olga Richard

THE H. W. WILSON COMPANY

NEW YORK · 1973

THE CHILD'S FIRST BOOKS

Library of Congress Cataloging in Publication Data

MAC CANN, DONNARAE.
    The child's first books.
Bibliography: p.   1. Illustrated books, Children's—History and criticism.
2. Picture-books for children.   3. Children's literature—History and criticism.
I. Richard, Olga, joint author.   II. Title.

Z1023.M25   741.64'2   73–3224
ISBN 0–8242–0501–4

Acknowledgments

This study was initiated with the assistance of the Dutton-Macrae Award, and
the authors wish to express appreciation for that early support. We are also
grateful for the encouragement and guidance of consultant Frances Clarke Sayers
and for the advice of the following critics and readers during the early stages of
this study: Robert Vosper, John Goodlad, Marjeanne Blinn, Carolyn Horovitz,
Elizabeth Herman, and Miriam Morton. Eugene Richard and Richard MacCann
have been continuously helpful as critics and supporters.

The authors acknowledge with gratitude the cooperation of the artists and publishers listed
below, who granted permission to reproduce illustrations from their books.
Color illustrations.   *Following page 32:*
From *Joanjo* by Jan Balet. Copyright © 1965 by Annette Betz Verlag. Copyright © 1967 by
Macdonald & Co. (Publishers) Ltd. A Seymour Lawrence Book/Delacorte Press. Reprinted by
permission of the publisher.   From *Birds* by Brian Wildsmith. Reprinted by permission of the
publishers: Oxford University Press; Franklin Watts, Inc.   From *Henri's Walk to Paris* by
Leonore Klein. Design & Illustration by Saul Bass & Art Goodman—Saul Bass & Associates.
Following page 64: From *Mr. Gumpy's Outing* by John Burningham. Copyright © 1970 by
John Burningham. Reproduced by permission of Holt, Rinehart and Winston, Inc. and of Jon-
athan Cape Ltd.   From *Madeline in London* by Ludwig Bemelmans, Copyright © 1961 by
Ludwig Bemelmans. All rights reserved. Reprinted by permission of The Viking Press, Inc.
and of Andre Deutsch Ltd.   Illustration by Maurice Sendak from *The Moon Jumpers* by
Janice May Udry. Picture Copyright © 1959 by Maurice Sendak. Reprinted by permission of
Harper & Row, Publishers.   From *Tikki Tikki Tembo* retold by Arlene Mosel. Illustrated by
Blair Lent. Copyright © 1968 by Blair Lent, Jr. Reproduced by permission of Holt, Rinehart and
Winston, Inc.
Black-and-white illustrations.   *Frontispiece:* Illustration from *Rapunzel* by Felix Hoffmann.

Black and White Illustrations

Color Illustrations

Contents

Preface

THE STORIES and illustrations in picture books can make a strong, positive contribution to a child's early education. When well conceived and well designed, such books reveal the delights of verbal and pictorial expression, suggest some of the nuances of human character, celebrate the achievements of the creative imagination, and display many of the varied wonders of nature. There is scarcely any limit to the diversity and aesthetic richness they can provide.

As part of the young child's environment, picture books can have a profound effect upon his whole pattern of development. Modern research has shown that some of the most important human characteristics are developed during the first five years of life. According to Benjamin Bloom of the University of Chicago, one crucial characteristic, general intelligence, develops most rapidly at the age of four. Another characteristic, general school achievement, has its most rapid development during the third grade, or when the child is approximately eight years of age (*Stability and Change in Human Characteristics*, Wiley, 1964).

For parents and others who educate children, the most important finding in Bloom's research is this: Environment has the greatest effect upon a characteristic during the period of its most rapid growth. Hence a child's first eight years must be thoughtfully and generously provided for. No cultural or intellectual deprivation must occur during this period if the child is to reach his full potential in later years.

The public has been slow to acknowledge the importance of preschool education or to supply needful facilities for it. But there are encouraging signs. Federal and state agencies are helping to support libraries, Head Start programs, and other activities that benefit the young child. Responding to the needs of the growing preschool audience, publishers are giving greater attention to the picture book, but often with more concern for quantity than quality. Our aim in this study is to focus attention on aesthetic quality and potential.

The authors define *picture book* as that distinctive type of publication in contemporary children's literature in which the written narrative is brief and the story line or other content is largely presented through illustrations. Nearly every scene, object, or idea is imparted to the reader visually as well as verbally. The picture book is a picture story in the purest sense, with much less space given to words than to illustrations.

A second kind of book has been included under the designation *picture book* even though the correlation between illustration and word content is slightly different. A profusely illustrated short story, in which care has obviously been taken in the selection of the artist and much space allotted to his work, is also referred to in this study as a picture book. In books of this kind, every scene will not have a corresponding illustration, the child will not be able to deduce the entire plot line from the pictures alone, yet the ratio of illustrations to text will be much higher than in most publications for children. There will be fewer illustrations than in the pure picture story, but they will be equally distinguished as works of art and clearly of great importance to the book as a whole. Examples of this latter type include elaborately illustrated folk tales or legends such as *Cinderella* (1954) illustrated by Marcia Brown and *Mazel and Shlimazel; or The Milk of a Lioness* (1967) illustrated by Margot Zemach.

This definition of the picture book, stressing the high coordination between illustration and word content, points up the distinction between the picture book as a genre in children's literature and the *illustrated book,* which may have many illustrations or decorations on its pages but still a clear predominance of text.

Physically, the two art forms, literature and graphic art, coexist comfortably within the picture-book format, for graphic art is, like the printed page, two-dimensional. But this convenient format may mislead one into judging both art forms by similar or identical criteria. If each art is not studied from the standpoint of its special and unique characteristics, there will be a tendency to ascribe the qualities of one to the other. This obscures the standards for both.

The emphasis in the following pages is upon *literary elements* and *graphic elements*, and they are usually discussed separately. Other components of bookmaking (typography, binding, and so forth) are taken into account, but they are not as critical to the book's essence and final impact. If either the writing or the graphic art is lacking in aesthetic quality, only a limited use can be made of the book. It is a defect of such large proportions that good librarians are forced to say: "Show it only as a piece of graphic art," or "Use this text for oral storytelling, but keep the book out of sight."

In reference to the picture-book audience, the authors use the terms *listener, reader, viewer* interchangeably. Most children during the early years of two to seven have not yet learned to read independently, but in addition to being listeners, they are such careful, exacting viewers of illustrations that their picture viewing is often loosely referred to by teachers and librarians as "reading." The semantics is not important, but it is helpful to remember that, for the most part, the picture-book audience is still lacking in reading skills and therefore needs stories presented orally or visually. At the same time, the child is capable of "reading" much more than the mere subject content of a picture. His responsiveness to mood and to a great diversity of graphic styles is remarkably broad and spontaneous.

Works dealing with books for children often try to provide guidance about age ranges. But in discussing picture books, the authors have avoided rigid age categories, simply indicating that preschool or primary-grade children have been a frequent and satisfied audience for some particular book. The youngest child, the two- to four-year-old, has a few special interests, but even this distinction should not be given undue weight. The picture book, with its brevity and visual emphasis, is almost by definition fitted to the young child's needs.

The major concern of this study can be summed up in these terms: The picture book offers an ideal opportunity to reach and delight children aesthetically at the very time when it will count the most. But this opportunity is circumscribed in various ways. Many books are not as good as they could be. To point out the malady is, hopefully, to hasten the cure.

At the same time, a body of good picture-book literature has gradually accumulated over the past seventy years, and this should be emphasized so that more children will have this literature offered to them in preference to inferior works. Literary criticism and art criticism serve this function and are important parts of this study.

Criticism is "not a carping, hair-splitting" activity, as James Reeves notes in *The Critical Sense; Practical Criticism of Prose and Poetry* (Hillary, 1964), but rather "the faculty of seeing, at least in part, *why* we enjoy something a great deal, and something else more, and something else less." The chapters in this study all have something to do with this "faculty of seeing . . . why"—why some qualities in picture books enhance the pleasure children find in them, other qualities detract, and others are a mixed blessing.

The author and critic Elizabeth Drew says that "the function of criticism is to send people to literature." It is in this spirit that the problems of the contemporary picture book are examined in these pages, for sending adults to children's literature is the quickest way we know to bring this literature to children.

Introduction: The Diminutive Bookman

Children express their artistic capacities and interests in many ways. They stroke an interesting surface, explore the graphic details in a picture, carry a variety of shapes in their pockets to feel and handle, beat time with a spoon, speak in metaphors, and devise rhythmic patterns with words and sounds. All such pastimes are spontaneous in the young child, natural activities which equip him for an ever-increasing appreciation of the "many particular beauties" of art.

In Peter and Iona Opie's book *The Lore and Language of Schoolchildren*, there are hundreds of examples of playful, rhythmic word games:

> It's a duck, it's a duck,
> Stuck in the muck, stuck in the muck.
>
> Roly poly barley sugar,
> Roly poly barley sugar.
>
> Queenie, Queenie Caroline,
> Dipped her hair in turpentine,
> Turpentine to make it shine,
> Queenie, Queenie Caroline.[1]

Children improvise dances—bobbing, turning, swaying—with total immersion in musical suggestions. Trudi Schoop, a renowned Swiss ballerina who had her own company, watched children improvise to music in an unstructured situation and noted that they used spontaneously and with amazing synthesis all the known ballet positions.

At the same time children are dramatists; they role-play energetically whether it involves "becoming" a wolf, a bear, or another person. This faculty is universal, however varied in levels of creativity. García Lorca's brother reports on the village childhood of the famous Spanish poet:

> How many times, as a game, he would pass whole hours talking like a maid in a rich house, like a little old convent lady, like a villager from Alpujarra. The exactness of the language, the intonation and characterization were prodigious. . . . It was not simple imitation but an untiring creation, conceived naturally, in its reality.[2]

The paintings and drawings made by young children in an unhampered environment show a wide range of responses to art elements. From busy, detailed (almost microscopic) minutiae, to flat, decorative, sometimes heavy patterning, to simple, quiet, line meanderings, children demonstrate highly individual methods of graphic performance. Creativity is shown in the different ways children use their picture plane space. They arrange shapes and colors to please their own sense of aesthetics. The child's behavior at the easel, whether he is using brush, pencil, ball-point pen, colored crayons, or other materials, is characterized by an involvement, lack of inhibition, and expressiveness which are the envy of many mature artists.

Not only do children perform with great variety, there is also differentiation in their acceptance of visual elements. They are quick in sensing and accepting a wide variation of style and expression. If Braque wants to cut reality up, reshape and reassemble it in his own grays and browns, this is perfectly agreeable to children. They marvel at his immense ingenuity. They know how difficult it is to think of many shapes and arrange them in a pleasing way, and yet many children are happiest and most involved when they are busy resolving similar aesthetic dilemmas.

If Miró forsakes landscape as we know it and suspends, in a kind of infinity, many clean-edged, wired-together forms which suggest the movement of a mobile, this is acceptable too. Children wonder at his precise, science-fiction-like innovations and his sense of color. Sheeler discards noise, smog, clutter, and even man from his urban scenes and builds his own many-windowed skyscrapers. At the school the authors are most familiar with, children not only accept this, they cheer and applaud and instantly recognize a Sheeler painting. "Sheeler's cities are so still and lonely, like they were brand new and no one has moved in yet." They think Marin's and Tobey's city paintings are crowded and "noisy-looking," the way cities really are. They understand that the artists intended to create these different impressions. One child remarked, "Why should Marin, Sheeler, and the other artists paint the same way? They're different people, and so they feel differently about things."

Looking at picture-book illustrations, a six-year-old noticed that the girl carrying the bucket in Frasconi's illustration in *The House That Jack Built* (1958) gave the feeling of being in "a big hurry." "There's a rushing feeling from the way the body is placed." "It leans on the edge of the paper." Marcia Brown's familiar portrait of Cinderella was seen as lonely, soft, gentle. "The colors are put on fuzzy." "The lines stop sometimes and that makes it soft too."

Evidence pointing to the aesthetic sensitivity of children can be gathered on all sides. They instinctively respond to balance, order, rhythm, originality—the artist's endless arrangements of color, line, shape, texture, and the writer's ingenious inventions and euphonies. But there are many exposures which can dwarf the natural growth of these responses. When the child is faced with a preponderance of inferior visual and literary impressions, a negative effect upon the development of taste and aesthetic enjoyment can be expected, as surely as a good effect can be predicted (all else remaining equal) when the child is surrounded by an artistic environment. He is not, after all, living in a vacuum.

Creating a beneficial environment for children is one of the most common objectives in education. Teachers and parents scrutinize the child and his surroundings with great care, trying to identify the activities which rouse curiosity and interest, which have strong and lasting effects and to which the child repeatedly returns. Yet they often overlook the arts or give them little emphasis, even when it is clear that few areas of experience involve children so completely and at such an instinctively high level.

Sometimes it is not a question of neglect but rather a problem of low standards: a cheap book from the supermarket serving as a "literary" experience, and a few art materials stored in a cupboard considered sufficient access to the plastic and graphic arts. For a higher standard, parents and teachers could look to Jacques Barzun's childhood as an enviable model. In his book *The Energies of Art* he describes

> The first picture seen: Cubist; the first music heard: Stravinsky's *Sacre*; the first poetry and drama: Futurist, Simultanist, 'experimental,' like the first building visited, which was Auguste Perret's 'modernistic' skyscraper apartment, Rue Franklin—all this, thanks to childhood's uncritical acceptance of the given as normal, could not help forming the most natural introduction to art as it is made.
>
> . . . it was Apollinaire interspersing his critical arguments for the grown-ups with stories for the child; it was Marie Laurencin amid her pictures telling the boy to sit still while she sketched him. . . .[3]

Such a close proximity of art works, artists, and children is obviously rare and difficult to plan. Yet it is possible to duplicate some of the essence of the situation. Within the picture book committed artists make available their visual statements; the child associates with such reputable painters as Ludwig Bemelmans and Hans Fischer and such an eminent woodcut artist as Antonio Frasconi. He has contact with what comes close to an original piece of fine art, for the graphic art of book illustration, as practiced by Frasconi and others, is a fine-arts medium. All the variables and potentialities of a graphic arts print have been taken into account in the creation of the illustration (the size and flatness of the page, the capacities of the printing press). The concept is free of confusion and the impact on the child is strong and clear, coming directly from an original artist.

Also within the picture book the child finds a stimulus for his literary instincts. He enjoys the dramatic form of good storytelling, the euphonies of language, the wit and ingenuity of the imagination, and the peculiar pleasure evoked by skillful character portrayal.

If he does not have the rare advantages of Jacques Barzun's childhood, he nevertheless has access to a considerable amount of visual and literary art through the picture book. And when the quality is high, the voice and vision of author and artist are no less pronounced, no less honest and refreshing, than those of an actual artist friend.

The child's response to quality picture books is that of an authentic, though diminutive, bookman. One four-year-old library patron was so attached to a book called *Katy and the Big Snow* (1943) that it was impossible to separate them; it would have caused a scene in the library, if not a trauma in the child. This fervor was not merely a sign of the possessiveness typical of young children; it was clearly a passion for a book—in this case the story of a heroic snowplow. *Horton Hears a Who* (1954), *Madeline* (1939), *Harry the Dirty Dog* (1956), and *The Tale of Peter Rabbit* (1902), to mention just a few widely shared favorites, have the same magnetic pull.

Lillian Smith, in her book about children's literature, designates the years of childhood as "the unreluctant years," and nowhere is this trait, this quick responsiveness, more noticeable than in the picture-book audience.[4] The young child freely gives to writers and artists the benefit of his unprejudiced mind. Yet specific qualities in the book determine whether his reaction will be strong or weak, positive or negative. Notwithstanding initial "unreluctance," an inept or insipid book creates boredom in a child as surely as it does in anyone else and may instill suspicion about the value of books in general. On the other hand, a marked devotion occurs when strong literary or graphic elements are present, when there are illustrations, incidents, characters, or modes of expression which prove intriguing. Then the child quickly involves himself in the drama of the action, identifies with the hero, immerses himself in the setting, mimics comic characters, chants rhythmic words and phrases, and examines illustrations with an amazing awareness of mood and detail.

A two- or three-year-old usually likes texts to be brief and simple, but aside from these obvious features, there are few limitations to a child's response to the arts. His capacity ranges over all kinds of subject matter and all types of literary and graphic forms.

The standards for picture books would be higher if writers, artists, publishers, and librarians paid more attention to the child's own artistic openness. Children constitute a "vast reservoir of impressionists who [do] very good work," wrote Ludwig Bemelmans. In his speech accepting the Caldecott prize for picture-book illustration, Bemelmans referred to his dissatisfaction with the conventional art market and then shared his estimation of the child audience:

I looked for another way of painting, for privacy; for a fresh audience, vast and critical and remote, to whom I could address myself with complete freedom. I wanted to do what seemed self-evident—to avoid sweet pictures, the eternal still lifes, the pretty portraits that sell well, arty abstractions, pastoral fireplace pictures, calendar art and surrealist nightmares.

I wanted to paint purely that which gave me pleasure, scenes that interested me; and one day I found that the audience for that kind of painting was a vast reservoir of impressionists who did very good work themselves, who were very clear-eyed and capable of enthusiasm. I addressed myself to children.[5]

1
Historical Perspective

Picture books as we know them today are a relatively recent publishing innovation, but the history of book illustration or book art extends back to ancient times. In many countries of the western world, book art preceded the art of easel or mural painting. In the Romanesque period, from A.D. 500 to 1150, illuminated manuscripts were decorated in lively, vigorous, and versatile styles. The Celtic monks of Ireland and northern England of around A.D. 700 were sometimes realistic in their book art, but often very geometric and fanciful, intricately decorating the page. Handmade books were among the most expressive and creative art products of the Middle Ages, and in France in the fourteenth and fifteenth centuries bookmaking reached a high point when, inspired by stained glass, artists used similar colors for exquisite and imaginative illustrations.

With the arrival of printing in Europe in the fifteenth century, type was used for a book's lower-case letters but blank spaces were left on the page for initials and marginal decorations to be added in color by hand. In general the effect was the same as in the manuscript.

Illustrations by important, well-known artists began to appear in printed books; Albrecht Dürer (1471–1528), for example, created woodcuts which were bold and imaginative. Also in Germany, Hans Holbein (1497–1543) first made his mark as an illustrator, using copper engraving to create some particularly memorable title pages.[1] In Spain Goya's powerful and expressive prints, *Caprichos* (1799), were published in book form, and in France Delacroix illustrated Goethe's *Faust* in 1828 using an autolithography process.

From 1860 to the present, nearly the entire art community of Paris has been involved in book art. With photography used in reproductions in books, the chasm widened between the experimentalists and traditionalists, with the latter group holding to a romantic representationalism, while the experimentalists innovated with new expressive visual ideas, new techniques, new forms and styles, and new aesthetic philosophies. The book became part of this involvement. So many artists have served as illustrators that the book can be considered a major contemporary consumer and vehicle of artistic expression. Arp, Barlach, Courbet, Daumier, Toulouse-Lautrec, Redon, Dufy, Picasso, Rouault, Matisse are only a few of the many artists who have enriched books with the same quality of genius that has distinguished their easel paintings. Picasso, undoubtedly our century's most prolific and creative genius in the arts, has done countless illustrations and graphics for books.

This level of creativity in illustration has not been the case historically in Great Britain or America, where the art of the book is considered a "minor" art, and where artists' accomplishments in illustrations have been, until recently, relatively mediocre. According to David Bland in *The Illustration of Books*, the English were at a disadvantage beside the French because the French had no inhibitions about using different graphic processes: "To combine letterpress and lithography did not seem a sin to them; but in England the cult of the wood-engraving was found to lead to formalism."[2] Another reason was the traditional aversion among English Protestants to the representation of religious subjects. The heritage was meager.

This is the background against which the reader should examine the history of the children's picture book. Illustrated books are not a recent innovation, but rather an established and respected art form. There was, however, less acceptance of the illustrator as an artist in England and America, where, even today, there is resistance to the artist participating freely in book art. When one places the early children's books in historical perspective, it becomes evident that the general tendency of the illustrations was within the conservative tradition.

The modern picture book for children was the product of Victorian England and owes much to Edmund Evans, one of England's foremost color printers in the 1860s and 1870s. It was Evans' idea to mass-produce books for young children, illustrated profusely and in color by well-known illustrators of his day. He introduced no new principles for color printing, but rather helped each artist understand the wood-engraving process and maximize its potential. After Evans himself had engraved the drawing made by the artist on wood, he sent the artist a proof to color in flat washes. Then Evans printed with oil colors which were very close to those used by the artist. The result was apparently far better than the usual color work of that period (chromolithographs which had a tendency to be gaudy).[3]

The forerunners of these books are important in the development of children's literature, but for the most part, they bear little resemblance to the picture book as Evans conceived of it. The *Orbis Pictus* or *Visible World* (1658) by John Comenius is commonly referred to as the first picture book, but it was more like an elementary type of encyclopedia. It consisted of 150 brief chapters on different topics with wood block illustrations, each object in the picture numbered and then identified by number in the text.

John Newbery (1713–1767) must be mentioned not because he contributed to picture-book literature per se, but because he changed the state of the children's book business. He gave it, for the first time, a firm, permanent foundation, separate from the field of adult publishing, and this affected all genres of children's books in the long run. With respect to format, it can be said that he initiated more pleasing book designs for children's books (flowery Dutch endpapers and gilt edging were notable features), but this was to sugar-coat the pill of moral instruction, the usual content in children's books in his era. Newbery did cater to the interests of children occasionally, as seen in his nursery rhyme collection *Mother Goose's Melody*, but he was more interested in the parent buyers and their approval of such fictionalized moral tracts as *The History of Little Goody Two-Shoes* (1766). In any case, his London shop, "The Sign of the Bible and the Sun," was profitable enough to place children in a new and permanent position as a market for books. This stimulated new activity from writers, educators, and publishers.

Thomas Bewick was the first great name in the history of illustrated children's books. He lifted the art of wood engraving to a high level in England, creating a new quality of tone and the simulation of varying textures.[4] In 1771 he created a book specifically for children, *The New Lottery Book of Birds and Beasts*, but some of his adult books undoubtedly pleased them just as much: *The History of Quadrupeds* (1790), *British Birds* (1797), and several books of fables.

William Blake illustrated several books for children (*Little Thumb and the Ogre* [1788], *Original Stories from Real Life* [1788] with a text by Mary Wollstonecraft, and *The Gates of Paradise* [1793]). His book *Songs of Innocence* (1789) also fell within a child's range, and had beautifully decorated, well-integrated pages.

Coming closer to the contemporary picture book in content were William Roscoe's *The Butterfly's Ball* (1807), Heinrich Hoffmann's *Struwwelpeter* or "Shock-headed Peter" (1845), and Edward Lear's *Book of Nonsense* (1846). These books are all pure entertainment. *The Butterfly's Ball* is a story in verse about an elegant social gathering of gnats, dragonflies, grasshoppers, butterflies, and so on. Illustrations were engravings after the manner of William Mulready, an important English academic artist of his day.[5] And one could purchase, as was customary in the early eighteen hundreds, a plain or a colored edition, the color applied by child labor.

Struwwelpeter (translated as *Slovenly Peter*) was the work of a young German doctor who was first of all trying to amuse his own three-year-old son, and in the second place trying to calm "the little antagonist [his child patient], dry his tears and allow the medical man to do his duty."[6] The book consists of nonsense verses about children with enormously exaggerated bad habits and bad manners.

Of all the forerunners of the modern picture book, Edward Lear's *Book of Nonsense* is the most important. His line illustrations are original and expressive, they are perfectly in tune with his text of zany limericks, and the limericks themselves were a landmark in nonsense verse in the nineteenth century.

Prior to the illustrators who worked on picture books as we know them today, important English cartoonists had worked on other kinds of children's books. For example, George Cruikshank illustrated *Grimm's Fairy Tales* (1824), and Sir John Tenniel, *Alice's Adventures in Wonderland* (1865). These Englishmen were not illustrating picture books, yet their work may have influenced Edmund Evans in his decision to use popular illustrators for his picture-book venture. In any case, Evans began with Walter Crane, a commercial designer.

Crane was apparently intrigued by Evans' experiment, for he worked on nearly forty books between the years 1865 and 1876. His technique was decorative, and he was concerned about the whole design of the book, its borders, lettering, and, unique at this time, double-page spreads.[7] However, his work has been criticized for being mechanical, repetitious, and sometimes lacking in good draftsmanship. He was a better art teacher than artist, for as one of his contemporaries noted, "He knows too much, and has not enough inspiration."[8] Traditional nursery rhymes and fairy tales constituted his textual material, beginning with *Sing a Song of Sixpence* (1866).

In 1878 Evans persuaded Randolph Caldecott, an artist who had contributed many illustrations to English periodicals, to succeed Crane. And like Crane, Caldecott illustrated traditional English nursery rhymes and songs for the most part—*The House That Jack Built* (1878), *The Frog He Would A-Wooing Go* (1883)—seventeen books altogether before his death in 1886. Leslie Brooke (an English illustrator of the twentieth century) spoke of Caldecott's talent as "an extreme instance of instinctive drawing"; and historians have referred to his artistic virility and his special suitability as an illustrator for children. He has been praised for "his natural sweetness and gaiety of spirit, all his love of life out-of-doors."[9] The American prize for each year's best-illustrated picture book is named for him: the Caldecott Medal.

Kate Greenaway was the third English artist to come under the persuasive influence of Evans. In 1878 she illustrated a collection of her own brief verses, *Under the Window,* and continued working for children both as a writer and illustrator for the rest of her life. Most critics agree that the less said about her verses the better, and some have taken a dim view of her illustrations as well. Quaintness is about their only notable feature. Still, they became so popular that by the 1890s "life had caught up with art," and parents began dressing their daughters to correspond with the drawings in the Greenaway picture books.[10] (These costumes were entirely Miss Greenaway's invention.)

Several important picture books were published in England around the turn of the century: William Nicholson's *An Alphabet* (1898), Beatrix Potter's *The Tale of Peter Rabbit* (1902), and Leslie Brooke's *Johnny Crow's Garden* (1903). Miss Potter's stories about Peter and other small woodland and domestic animals are uneven in the quality of their illustrations, but for the most part they are exceptionally well written. Leslie Brooke's Johnny Crow books are still widely enjoyed for their comic animal characters, but only the Nicholson book has lasting importance for its graphic art. Nicholson's *Alphabet* is a series of woodcuts which were colored by hand in the original editions and reproduced by lithography for the mass-produced editions. The artist had studied in Paris and had been influenced by Toulouse-Lautrec and other painters; as was common in France, he did not consider it beneath his dignity to prepare his own printing surfaces.[11]

In America children enjoyed the English picture books soon after they were published, and there were a few American contributions to the genre at the end of the nineteenth century. The first Brownie book appeared in 1887: *The Brownies, Their Book*. This was the beginning of a series of nine books by Palmer Cox about mischievous, elf-like characters who were depicted as cowboys, policemen, Dutchmen, Frenchmen, and other types and nationalities. *A Book of Cheerful Cats and Other Animated Animals* (1892) by J. G. Francis was a nonsense picture book with brief verses accompanying very expressive line drawings. E. Boyd Smith created a number of books in the early 1900s: *The Chicken World* (1910) was one of the best, a book depicting the seasons of the year as well as chicken-yard life.

These picture-book artists in England and America can be viewed as competent cartoonists and draftsmen for the most part. Kate Greenaway is an exception because she was not a good draftsman (even her friend, John Ruskin, severely criticized her on this score). William Nicholson is an exception because he was much better than the others, and his *Alphabet* was only incidentally a children's book. But in general the first picture-book illustrators were representative of the commercial art world of their day. As key figures in the history of the picture book, Crane, Caldecott, and Greenaway should not be underestimated, but taking the larger perspective of art history, we see movements underway to which they had little relation.

Histories of children's literature have usually not attempted to show a relationship between children's book illustration and art history in general. But it is helpful to consider picture books from this perspective. Then it is evident that the illustrators who created the first picture books are not the same artists who made a long-range impact aesthetically. Unless this distinction is clear, nineteenth century picture books can exert a disproportionate influence on present-day taste.

In France in the early 1800s the visual arts were undergoing enormous changes in direction. The artist, isolated from the comfort of royal patronage, became highly individualistic and personal in his approach. At the same time, the artist's new patron, the growing middle class, was preoccupied with business, politics, and other pressing problems of the new democratic society. The businessman looked to the past for his aesthetic standards and was most comfortable with naturalistic depictions of history, romance, or moral conduct. Thus, two directions were indicated to the artist: He could emulate the naturalism and traditional stylization which were understood by the new middle-class art buyer, or, if this was not palatable to him, he could isolate himself by rebelling. And rebel he did. By the latter half of the nineteenth century he had created not only new forms, but new aesthetic concepts. He distorted, innovated, experimented, explored light, utilized new materials; he discovered art forms of the Far East and Africa and incorporated these into his canvases, and in many other ways revolutionized the art styles of his time.

Among the artists who participated in this revolt and search were Delacroix, Rousseau, Corot, Millet, Daumier, Manet, Monet, Picasso, Sisley, Renoir, Cézanne, Degas, Gauguin, Van Gogh, Matisse, Toulouse-Lautrec, and Seurat. Similar innovations occurred in Germany to create Expressionism, which produced such artists as Kollwitz, Liebermann, Slevogt, and Corinth.

America in the nineteenth century was also in a period of great economic and social change. The frontier unfolded, industrialization expanded, Jacksonian democracy developed the concept of the common man, but American art was submerged in provincialism. The artist took his directions from the English school, and collectors approved only the European products of art which sprang from an earlier age.

In the 1870s, six remarkable painters lifted American art out of provincialism: Whistler, Inness, Martin, Eakins, Homer, and Ryder. They were not popular; their varied tonalism and interest in mood, drama, and intensity were above the level of current tastes. From 1875 on, American art felt the full force of the French influence, first the Impressionists, and later the Expressionists, Cubists, and other Postimpressionists. The Parisian idiom became acceptable to the American artist, and an intense and varied art resulted. The list of creative talents is large: Weber, Halpert, Karfiol, Marin, Kuhn, Brook, Kuniyoshi, Kantor, Sheeler, Demuth, O'Keeffe, and many others.

Children's picture books were little affected by these advances until the First World War and its aftermath. The European upheaval caused a number of artists to flee their native countries and take up residence in the United States. This influx of talented refugees is probably the single most important circumstance in the history of the American picture book. In the hands of such artist-immigrants as Fritz Eichenberg, Boris Artzybasheff, Jan Balet, Feodor Rojankovsky, Roger Duvoisin, Georges Schreiber, Ludwig Bemelmans, Nicholas Mordvinoff, and others, the picture book received an impetus which gave it, for the first time, a graphic as well as a literary importance. It emerged somewhat from the conservative confinement of the nineteenth century.

The steady flow of European artists to America after 1920 added to the already diversified racial background of Americans, and the effect this had on children's picture books cannot be stressed enough. As the book historian David Bland writes about this development:

The category [of graphic art] that has been most influenced is the one which was able to benefit most, the child's book; and it is here that the best contemporary American work is often to be seen.[12]

The United States became, therefore, the meeting ground for two major traditions important to children and their literature. On the one hand there was

16

the British tradition, since John Newbery's time, of designing and publishing books especially for children (and, after Edmund Evans, designing many in color). On the other hand, the extensive variety of European art, the strong European folk art tradition, and the influence of Impressionism and Expressionism found their way into the American picture book through many distinguished artist-immigrants.

Understanding these trends has more than a purely academic significance. Illustrations by Greenaway, Caldecott, Crane, and other nineteenth century artists have been publicized in a manner out of proportion to their actual importance in art history. This has given some critics an inordinate fondness for one or two conventional styles and imitations of these styles.

Acquaintance with the various movements in art, and corresponding developments in book art, will help the critic appreciate a wide range of styles in contemporary illustration. Then as picture books are appraised and honored each year, the prize-winning books (especially the Caldecott award winners) will be those which are actually contributing to art history. They will not represent only the conservative tendencies.

The proliferation of twentieth century art is such that both avant-garde and kitsch flourish simultaneously. Action painting, surrealism, abstract expressionism, pop art, op art, minimal art, figurative art, process art, formalist art, micro-painting, multimedia work, representational art—this multiplicity of styles may be visually abrasive when viewed out of context, that is, outside the framework of culture and period. But it is still incumbent on the viewer to understand the idiom of his age, as Théophile Gautier warned in 1850:

> To be of one's own time—nothing seems easier and nothing is more difficult. One can go straight through one's age without seeing it, and this is what has happened to many eminent minds.[13]

2

Stereotypes
in Illustration

W~HEN~ the picture-book buyer enters a bookstore today, he is usually confronted with rack upon rack of glossy-covered "flats," picture books containing some of the worst stereotypes in art. Library patrons have better books to choose from, but even here inferior illustrations are often the rule rather than the exception. Only part of this inferiority stems from inadequate craftsmanship; the rest has its roots in stereotyped concepts.

Stereotyped illustrations are easy to spot once their principal earmarks are pointed out. The illustrator is usually conforming to derivative criteria. He duplicates a formula already known and familiar to himself and to the consumer. Objects are altered, but in a schematic way that is traditional in books for children. Animals are either anthropomorphized or drawn so that they resemble their stuffed-toy counterparts. Children and adults are drawn in costumes designed to defy period labeling; little girls have very full skirts and boys have short pants or are schematized in some similar fashion. The individualization of characters is accomplished by a cartoon-like overstatement of features. This kind of alteration is not concerned with aesthetic enrichment or emphasis.

The problem was summed up in an issue of the *Times Literary Supplement* in 1933: "It is a well-established habit of illustrators to give every animal and figure a soft and kittenish charm, on the hypothesis that the qualities in children which appeal to adults will appeal to children in everything else."[1] Or another way to perceive the problem is to see that "sweetness," as illustrator Nicholas Mordvinoff says, has often been used as a "substitute for feeling and intelligence." He continues with these apt comparisons:

Sweet [is] the calendar scene with a willow, but not the poplar trees in Van Gogh's painting; the apron-clad kittens on the greeting card, but not the cats of Goya; the pink babies on advertising posters, but not the children of Velásquez. . . .[2]

In the stereotyped illustration, the traditional use of line has been to outline an object in uniform blackness. The effect is quite similar to that of the coloring book: The outline marks the boundaries of the colors used. Occasionally line is used to suggest movement, but in a cartoon-strip style. Color is usually flat, closely related to the object depicted and reflecting the commonly held notion that children respond only to primary hues. Texture is limited to fuzziness, fatness, or frilliness. The same technique is used for the achievement of each kind of texture: shortening or lengthening the uniform stroke of the pen or pencil. Plumpness is suggested by exaggerated shape in the face, cheeks, and abdominal area, and also by shadows on the sides of each individual object, drawn so that a sausage-like roundness ensues. Relatively little attention is devoted to the spatial arrangement of the objects on the page. The "center of interest" is drawn large, outlined heavily, and made brighter in color, while the other objects are relegated to a subordinate position by the simple process of diminishing size and color, and placing the objects off to the side of the page.

This stereotyped method of illustrating has the broadest public acceptance, for it is the most familiar. However, there is also a fairly wide following for the illustrations that represent a middle ground between the creative artist and the mere hack. These illustrations are produced by professionals whose talent, skill, and training enable them to function as artistic mediators. They may be compelled less by expressive or interpretive needs than by commercial success and the publisher's requirements. Yet this pseudo-artistic posture as mediator between the creative artist and the public is not a delegated role. It is an assumed one. The pseudo-artist astutely appraises both the real artist's work and the public level of acceptance, and then borrows just enough of the creative artist's innovations to be acceptable to the public. In fact, he becomes more than acceptable; he is often more richly rewarded for this sleight-of-hand than the original artist from whom he borrows.

The situation is perfectly understandable. The public resists change, but at the same time it is bored with repetitive similarities. This dilemma is evaluated and manipulated by the pseudo-artist. He borrows from the creative artist some of the surface manifestations of creativity and reworks them by combining them with the traditional. This is the characteristic aura of the marketable, commercial "moderne" or "modernistic" object, whether it be a picture-book illustration or mass-produced furniture.

Several mannerisms are typically exploited by the lesser artist in the picture book. Take, for example, the creative artist's emphasis upon spontaneity and his respect for the spontaneity of the young child's painting. The lesser artist has translated this to mean "paint and draw like the child" and has utilized such child-like (and often inept) drawings in picture books. When this sham is added to the traditional arrangement and use of color, the aesthetic result is vulgarly inappropriate.

Expressive and personal qualities are lacking in most cheap picture books. The artist's intent is unclear. There is no involvement with any art element to

20

the point of emphasis. The artist is not a realist, for his concern has been with a formula, not a reality which he can translate; nor has he abstracted his concept for the purpose of furthering a mood, of strengthening color, or developing pattern with line. The language of art really does not concern him, only the expediency of the formula.

In addition to surface mannerisms in traditional illustrations, the public will often accept a change in the style of a picture achieved through innovations in picture size, paper color, and so on. An extreme example is the inclusion of three-dimensional game gimmicks. Since the public is receptive to demonstrations of technical skill in any field, it responds to these novelties, often without applying any other criteria.

The artistic inferiority represented in such books will not benefit the child, who is largely free from stereotypes and limiting visual conceptions during the picture-book years. Ben Shahn noted in a lecture at Harvard in 1957, "The popular eye is not *un*trained; it is only wrongly trained—trained by inferior and insincere visual representations."[3] Good picture books provide the opportunity to begin right.

The characteristics of the distinguished picture book are examined in detail in succeeding chapters. Every book is an artist's resolution of a specific problem in a specific manner. The specific problem is the subject matter of the book—the text—and the artist resolves this problem by carefully selecting those images he will develop. He decides which elements of art will best suit his ideas, whether he will emphasize color or line, texture or shape. He decides what arrangement of these elements will best express his aesthetic intentions. The choice of tools and the manner of utilizing them often become the artist's trademark and show his preference for a certain way of working, such as in woodcut or lithograph. Style, and a particular emphasis or interpretation, stem from the artist's individual personality.

The expressive quality of an illustration is the critical factor. Two artists may have similar interests in color, texture, and content, and yet one piece of work will have a quiet feeling and the other will seem closer to a roar. The emphasis applied to the content or text, the use of materials, or a chosen manner of distortion—any of these may serve as expressive means for the artist. By one means or another, the final result is a work impossible to imitate.

The picture-book critic must sense the uniqueness of the artist's visual world. This level of appreciation is the most difficult to achieve, for it is similar to understanding the subtle nuances of another personality without letting one's own personality obstruct the view.

3

Graphic Elements

Since the very inception of the picture book as a genre, the book critics' silence about visual content has been a serious problem. Typical reviewers shy away from critical comments on illustrations, or else they repeat only a few generalities. This silence has allowed stereotyped illustrations, both the old-fashioned and the "mod" varieties, to flourish and remain unchallenged.

The best way to encourage better criticism is to study closely and separately the graphic and literary elements in children's books. The criteria by which literature and the visual arts are judged are not the same. Both the writer and the illustrator create imagery of one kind or another, but the sets of "rules" within which writer and illustrator work are different. No one is more aware of this than the artist himself. The image he is trying to evoke must be created within a specific art form—with language if he writes and with colors, shapes, lines, and textures if he paints.

Illustrators work within the boundaries of the visual arts; they depend upon art elements that are seen, and the ability of their art to communicate depends upon the sensory responses of the audience. In order to evaluate picture-book illustrations, criteria must be found therefore in the graphic arts. Any consideration of illustration as less than art suggests that illustration lacks meaning in the very area it utilizes for communication—the visual.

There might appear to be an easier way to evaluate picture books. After all, it has been suggested, children are unknowing; they merely "read" the pictures anyway. Thus if the story is about a bear and his adventures in the woods, all that is required of illustrations is that the bear be a recognizable bear. This criterion is based on the false premise that the subject content of the picture is all that children perceive when they look at an illustration. Actually the child's eyes, more than the adult's, see the whole of the artist's statement. Untutored, unaware of fashion or fad, the child's eyes take in all that the page offers.

Object recognition is the easiest standard for judging illustrations. And there are historical precedents for this utilitarian approach. For years, illustrators have used their art to define and describe objects for encyclopedias (wild flowers, fossils, birds, and the like). Technical books in the fields of science, medicine, mechanics, or more commonplace how-to-do-it books use illustrations to describe what is in the text.

The picture-book illustrator has a quite different function. For him there is no point in trying to be purely representational. The meaning in his picture comes from the way he arranges colors, lines, shapes, and textures into a special synthesis, one that will please the senses and provide an aesthetic experience for the reader. Object recognition is a criterion based on the commonplace. It is concerned with simple imitation. The arts are the very antithesis of commonplace standards of imitation, recognition, and the sense of familiarity derived from such considerations.

It is obvious that the critic must make a special effort, both intellectual and emotional, if he is to accept this viewpoint. He must see that the pictorial statements are intended to add to, rather than merely describe, the text. The illustrations have an entity of their own, a quality within the visual area which adds another dimension to the perception of the book. This dimension is one of visual interpretation and the expression of the intrinsic nature of the text.

In *Henri's Walk to Paris* (1962), for example, everything is planned with skill and style. Objects, people, architecture—all are reduced to an interesting shape or color or line and arranged on the page to provoke visual interest. The illustrator, Saul Bass, compels our eyes to move and to cover what he intends us to cover. On one page he directs our eyes up from a flat-shaped soup pot with broken yellow steam lines. We follow the direction to four windowpane squares of green, lushly textured foliage and up to a white, flat bird. When we return to the pot of soup we pause to visually hop the row of bright, flat flower-shapes at the bottom of the picture.

On every page Bass gives the book a visual meaning of its own, apart from the story and the world of appearances and yet very much within both. He changes objects to create a new life for them and to entice our eyes.

In *The Moon Jumpers* (1959), the illustrations build a mood that is an individual artist's response to the writer's suggestions about playing outdoors at night. Maurice Sendak is not concerned with depicting a certain child in a certain environment. His concern is for a synthesis of colors, for light and dark contrast and the contrast of shapes and textures which together carry a quiet, mysterious feeling of the night world. The pictures by themselves accomplish this task. Every full-page illustration has a slightly haunted quality because of the way Sendak has combined visual elements.

Picture books are often chosen on the basis of a purely personal reaction: "I like it" or "I don't like it." Such acceptance or rejection is sometimes based simply on familiarity. An illustration may remind the reader of another picture with which a pleasant feeling has been associated in the past. In this case, it is the memory and pleasant association which is liked, rather than the illustration itself. A book about a cute, cartoon-like elephant, for example, may be a pleasant reminder of another elephant book associated with some warm childhood experience. This kind of liking is not, of course, an aesthetic judgment.

Personal taste should be supplemented by a consideration of the elements which contribute to the picture's effectiveness. Otherwise one might reject a sensitive illustration only because it is not in color. On such a basis, the simplicity of a thin line drawing, such as in Reiner Zimnik's *Jonah the Fisherman* (1956), would be rejected in favor of the full and stunning color of Deborah Ray's *The Winter Picnic* (1970). This is all right provided one knows what miracles are performed by Zimnik's brilliant little line. But very often color illustrations are preferred to line illustrations merely because they give more immediate satisfaction. Knowing this, many publishers use color to cover and gild inferior pictorial concepts and make them more salable. (This is not, however, the case with the beautiful Ray book, with its baroque richness and varied patterns.)

Again, one might prefer simple, flat, clean-edged areas of color to heavily textured, animated surfaces. If so, the purchaser of a children's book may un-

Low *Adam's Book of Odd Creatures*

consciously prefer Paul Rand or Jan Balet to Antonio Frasconi as illustrator. But he would need to establish this as a sincere commitment to personal aesthetics, not a rejection of a new and relatively unfamiliar style. If he hastily rejects an unfamiliar style, he is missing the chance to grow in his appreciation of art, and he is depriving the child as well.

To understand more about good illustrations, the critic should attempt to relate himself to the artist's intention. He can determine, by careful examination, which of the art elements the artist was emphasizing, whether color, line, texture, or shape. By rethinking the work of art in this way, the viewer will begin to understand the image he thinks he sees.

Take Joseph Low's books *Smiling Duke* (1963) and *Adam's Book of Odd Creatures* (1962) as examples. One marvels over the varied ways Low achieves the feeling of texture in the feathers and fur of his "odd creatures." The yak, zebu, wombat—all the fishes, birds, and bugs have different surface treatments. Close scrutiny of the lines reveals the secret of Low's style. How does he invest the creatures with such vitality? They are so animated, so alive. Is it because of the color? Look at the quagga and imagine it without the color. No, it would still have its vital quality. The secret is in the line, in the many directions the line takes, and the many textures made possible through line variation.

It is profitable to review illustrations in this way because the artist's interpretation gradually becomes more apparent. The original creative process involves conceptualizing, screening, choosing, ordering, organizing, and finally producing an illustration so that the external image may reflect the internal concept. This illustration is what we see, and the more closely we look, the more we are able to understand of the artist's special style.

Academic, Realistic, and Trompe l'Œil

The more directly the artist concerns himself with the task of representing objects in his illustrations, the easier it is to identify his intent. For example, he may not be interested in translating the way he feels about the sea, but only in using traditional ways of showing the sea in his pictures. There are many visual motifs which mean "sea" to everyone, in much the same way that the word does. Art of this sort does not copy nature, but copies a copy that has become a traditional symbol. This kind of art is free of emotional implications, since it is not a personal interpretation of the subject. It conforms to the rules of representation by being impersonal and restrained in manner. It is often slick, smooth, and technically expert in the use of imitative symbols. Such art in the traditional manner will be referred to as *academic*.

The objection to academic representational art is not that it is noncreative and so alien to the essence of art. Leo Steinberg, in *The Eye Is Part of the Mind*, suggests a more pertinent consideration when he says that a capacity for imitation "implies what no one seriously believes: that nature confronts man with a fixed, invariant look." Skill in copying usually presupposes that "the model's appearance is an objective fact susceptible of mechanical reproduction" when the

26

Rojankovsky *Animals in the Zoo*

truth is that "nature presents every generation (and every person . . .) with a unique and unrepeated facet of experience."[1]

When an artist is free from the academic tradition but wants to represent the life around him through his own special perception, he is termed *realistic*. The value of a realistic art work does not depend on the object portrayed, but on the manner in which the artist has made an expressive visual statement.

Contemporary artists Ben Shahn, Andrew Wyeth, and Leonard Baskin are all classified as realists. Ben Shahn categorized himself a "personal realist," and said that "both subjective and objective, . . . the image and the idea" were important to him, and that the "challenge is to unite them into an image of which meaning is an inalienable part." He stated in another book, however, that "the painter who stands before an empty canvas thinks in terms of paint, for his inner images are paint images."[2] Andrew Wyeth feels that getting to know the "pungency" of the object is the significant thing. "You have to feel it," he says. "Realism without emotion is dead painting."[3] Leonard Baskin also calls himself a realist "in the sense of one who communicates ideas, notions, feelings and beliefs about life."[4] Although Shahn, Wyeth, and Baskin all call themselves realists,

27

their paintings have nothing in common. It can be argued that they are not faithful to the object, that they distort and take liberties in interpretation. This is the quality that separates the realist from the academician: The art of the realist is nonrepeatable and personal; the realist adds his interpretation and feelings, whereas the academician copies with no concern for interpretation.

There is another kind of painting in which the artist is concerned with depicting objects in a most exact way. His intent is so to control his materials and

Ray *Frog, Frog, Frog*

28

techniques that the symbol on the paper duplicates the original exactly and one is moved to brush a painted insect off the canvas. This kind of painting is called *trompe l'œil*, and is intended literally to deceive the eye.

There are not many artists working in this manner now, nor have there ever been. Artists often draw objects with great accuracy as a disciplinary task, but they are demonstrating visual and technical aptitudes in much the same way as a musician spends hours with exercises at the piano. Such exercises serve secondary purposes. Artists fill countless sketch pads, but a study of paintings done from these sketches indicates that most artists change or alter the object in order to give it a personal interpretation.

Unfortunately, it is easier to find examples of the academic and traditional illustrator in children's picture books than examples of the realist who is searching for the "pungency" of the object he is interpreting. The academicians use standard symbols which have been imitated dozens of times. For example, to suggest *house* a cube is drawn, a triangle (roof) is placed atop this cube, and a long slim rectangle (chimney) rests against the side of the cube, extending beyond the triangle. The cube has a series of smaller squares drawn on its surface to represent windows and doors. Symbols which are more personal as to meaning, mood, and organization are less frequent in picture books.

There are, however, a few outstanding examples of realistic art in children's books. Adrienne Adams accomplishes her realistic task with line, carefully drawing the forms of architecture and people in *The Shoemaker and the Elves* (1960). Her *Snow White and Rose Red* (1964) is also impeccably drawn with the same controlled, serene line and detail, although here she designs more liberally than in *Shoemaker*. Feodor Rojankovsky's concern for the object sometimes approaches that of the artist working in a trompe l'œil manner. In a double page showing a measuring cup and a funnel in *So Small* (1962), there is such detail that the illusion of the funnel is most convincing. Illustrations in this book range from careless sketches to this precise definition of objects, an unfortunate unevenness. *Animals in the Zoo* (1962) is more consistent, with vari, kangaroo, jackrabbit, and hippopotamus especially successful in their realistic detail.

Lynd Ward fills the pages of *The Biggest Bear* (1952) with mural-like realism. One notable example is the page where a sculptured farmer stands behind high stalks of corn. Elsewhere Ward draws a bottle of maple syrup so convincingly that it needs only color to give the illusion a trompe l'œil, finger-licking sensation. Clare Newberry's *Pandora* (1944) shows a realist's concern for the shapes, textures, and mannerisms of the cat. Her scratchy pen-and-ink drawings are skillful and sensitive interpretations. Barbara Cooney's interests in *Chanticleer and the Fox* (1958) are those of the realist also. In her black-and-white drawing of Chanticleer and the hens, although the page is decorative, she appears most concerned with the appearance of the feathered bird mass.

Deborah Ray's skillful techniques are used within the realist's framework. In *Frog, Frog, Frog* (1971) she uses brown line in sensitive and gentle portraits which include a mother, her two small sons, and many frogs. Sometimes her line is softly textured, sometimes it is a simple contour, and often it is crisp and tightly patterned. Roger Duvoisin, in books like *Veronica* (1961), brings a fanciful decorator-interest to his depiction of objects, especially when he works with line. Robert McCloskey deals in several books with the realities of the seascape. *Burt Dow, Deep-Water Man* (1963) is a showcase for his talents in symbolizing animals, humans, hillside homes, and the sea. He also demonstrates his designer skills in dealing with shape and pattern in several very bold illustrations.

Abstract Art

There are countless individual means by which an artist can accomplish changes or alterations in his pictures. But he can alter the visual symbol only through the avenues of his craft. This means that he can change the color of the objects depicted, the shapes and sizes of the objects, the lines or textures, or the arrangement on the page. He can distort perspective, send color into remote areas, or flatten the entire picture plane. The only limitations are those imposed by a specific text and by his craft; he cannot alter his statement by means of any language but the visual one. He uses color, line, shape, texture; and he must arrange these elements in a limited space and with a sense of unity and synthesis. For purposes of identification, this mode of expression—where changes in objects have been made deliberately—is termed *abstract* art.

The scope of this style is vast. The artist's intent and the limits of his ingenuity determine the degree of abstraction. For an example of how this operates, one can visualize an apple, determining its kind, shape, size, color, and texture. If we draw several apples on a sheet of paper, the problem of arrangement automatically becomes a consideration. One must decide if the apples are to be in the center of the page, massed together, or grouped in various places. If we draw a single apple we can alter its shape. We can make it rounder, not by thinking of a different kind of apple, but by deliberately causing a change in the original symbol decided upon for the apple shape. We can make several round shapes overlap, or alter the shapes by elongating the forms or by using dozens of close, short, straight lines, rather than curvilinear ones, to indicate contour.

There are literally hundreds of alterations which can be made in the original apple symbol while still retaining enough of the "appleness" quality for identification. One artist's desire to use color results in color abstractions which are far removed from the original apple color. Another artist may become involved in patterning his colors and shapes. The alterations and combinations are innumerable, limited only by the artist's predisposition to this style of art.

There are many examples of this kind of abstraction in picture books. Jacob Lawrence, in *Harriet and the Promised Land* (1968), distorts to heighten meaning. He makes Harriet's hand larger than her body and extends it forward on the picture plane. In this way it relates more to the endless floor boards than to the body of which it is a part. Ed Young, in *Chinese Mother Goose Rhymes* (1968), places small decorative shapes within the larger shapes, breaking them up with a turquoise line and with occasional bright color spots. In *Umbrella* (1958), Taro

Lawrence *Harriet and the Promised Land*

Yashima builds form with light and dark contrasts that have nothing to do with real shadows. They are his own inventions.

Nonobjective Art

The artist of the twentieth century has moved increasingly away from the object in his painting. In fact many artists have moved from realistic to abstract renderings and then, captivated by the immense freedom and potential when the object loses its identity, have decided to eliminate the object completely.

Artists working within this frame of reference are *nonobjective* artists. The nonobjective artist uses color, line, shape, and texture in arrangements which are often charged with expressiveness or, conversely, suggest an ordering of elements that is serene and classical in feeling. Franz Kline said of his paintings,

31

"[I paint] not the things I see but the feelings they arouse in me." His concern is that his work be as expressive as possible, and, if a canvas "doesn't have imagery or emotion, I paint it out and work over it until it does."[5] But the suggestion must be made without any referent in the real world. If the viewer is looking at a nonobjective painting and trying to find the real world mirrored, he will be disappointed. But if he will accept the arranged canvas of color, line, shape, and texture as reality also—aesthetic reality—he has moved in the direction of an appropriate response.

Although most illustrations in children's books depict recognizable objects, many of these objects have been changed to give a stronger visual impact. Thus we find abstraction to be a rather general phenomenon. For the same reason, to create a more expressive content, artists will sometimes create a nonobjective background for these abstracted objects. Paul Rand deliberately plays with the elements of art in *Sparkle and Spin* (1957), designing with an interplay between the known object and the imagined shapes and colors. Leo Lionni, in *Little Blue and Little Yellow* (1959), is completely nonobjective in his torn-paper, collage-like illustrations; and Marianne Richter is more concerned with the design and texture of a wastebasket in the book *The Little Hedgehog* (1959) than with its narrative importance.

These general categories (academic, realistic, abstract, and nonobjective) allow us to identify loosely the artist's style and further extend our own awareness of the visual arts. When an illustration is identified as abstract, it is not appropriate to argue about whether or not there is distortion. Obviously there is, and once it is recognized, appropriate considerations deal with the qualities gained because of the distortion, such as a greater sense of color or design, or a feeling of activity, busyness, and so on.

An artist does not start out by placing himself in one of these categories. Personality factors make him more suited to one manner of painting and illustrating than another. Categories are, at best, sterile indices for understanding anything as complex as the individual artist and his work.

Historical Influences: Impressionism and Expressionism
Sometimes groups of artists within a special cultural climate develop styles which have long-lasting influences on artists in other countries. The French Impressionists (Pissarro, Monet, Degas, Renoir, among others), in the middle and late nineteenth century, worked within the landscape of the real world but decided to break up their colors and shapes to get an impression of light and airy atmosphere. These artists deliberately chose certain subjects in nature which would better demonstrate the quality of changing light and the feeling of space and air. Trees and bushes massed together, for example, can illustrate qualities of light more readily than the horizontal lines of faraway plains and sky.

Many excellent picture-book illustrators have this same interest in the quality of broken light, and alter their subject matter to achieve this quality. Maurice Sendak, in *Mr. Rabbit and the Lovely Present* (1962), achieves the illusive

Wildsmith *Brian Wildsmith's Birds*

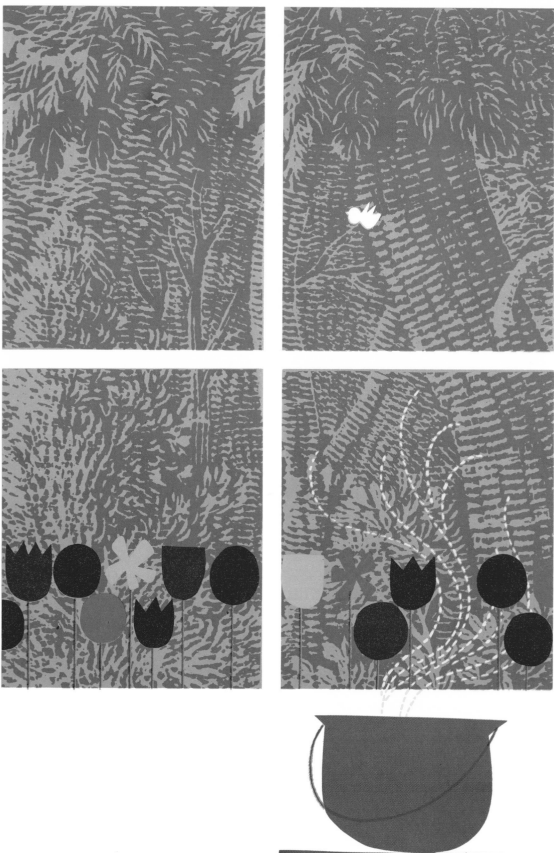

Bass *Henri's Walk to Paris*

and shimmering quality of broken light in illustrations reminiscent of the Impressionists' paintings.

The Expressionist movement represents another style with far-reaching influence. It overlapped the Impressionist movement and had its main development in Germany, although as a mode of expression it was felt simultaneously on much of the European continent. Van Gogh, Gauguin, Munch, and Kollwitz all worked in an Expressionist manner.

The Expressionists placed a priority on the individual's personal response, a response which was often in the nature of a protest. They often distorted objects violently, used raw and shocking colors, and exploited depressing themes in order to achieve a quality of intensity. The artist's manner of handling the color is often part of the technique of the Expressionist. In the brushwork of Van Gogh, for example, there are short, thick, overlapping brush strokes which create a textured surface extremely animated and dynamic in feeling.

Expressionist illustration is abundant. Fritz Eichenberg in his ABC book *Ape in a Cape* (1952) permeates his characters with Expressionistic animation. His treatment of light and dark, especially in the hands and head of the ape, gives the page a tense and dramatic quality. The children's book is a fertile field for the artist interested in infusing his art with emotional meaning. Children's books are full of imagery, a needed ingredient for the Expressionist artist, and there is also, in the Expressionist style, an affinity for the child's own spontaneity and uninhibited joy in art. Abe Birnbaum captures some of this fresh, alert spontaneity in *Green Eyes* (1953). The feeling he creates, with bold, uninhibited color, line, and arrangement, is not unlike the direct paintings made by young children. Ivan Chermayeff achieves a similar quality in his *Peter Pumpkin* (1963).

These two movements, Impressionist and Expressionist, still exert powerful influences in all areas of the visual arts. The energies released by the painters of the middle and late nineteenth century are still generating world-wide motivation for change. But the multiplicity of styles in the contemporary scene makes it difficult to produce an accurate inventory. Art shows quickly become testimonies of a style which may die the following year. The modes of the academicians, Impressionists, and Expressionists still persist, but must share exhibit space and influence with Rauschenberg's Coke bottles and Warhol's soup cans.

The Elements of Art*

The elements of art can be thought of as anything the artist uses as a means to an end: for example, color, shape, line, texture, and the arrangement of these components within a specified picture plane. Just as an artist seems to fit one category better than another (that is, he seems more of an abstract painter than a realist), so does an artist often emphasize one of the art elements more than

* Categories of elements vary, as does the emphasis placed on each element by different authors. Gyorgy Kepes, for example, uses color, value, texture, shape, direction, size, and interval as his meaningful units. The authors have chosen color, line, shape, texture, and composition because of the child's response in interpreting and using these elements.

the others. This is not to say that color is better than line, or texture better than differentiated shapes. No hierarchy is established except that, by the artist's choice, he emphasizes some elements more than others, and perhaps finds a greater usefulness in certain elements for the interpretation of certain texts.

Color

Many people can distinguish only nine colors: red, yellow, blue, green, orange, purple, black, brown, and white. Red-oranges and rich pinks are called "red"; blue-greens and yellow-greens are put into a "green" category, since there is a lack of sensitivity to the range of shades and mixtures possible. On the other hand, a seven-year-old in an elementary school once made a painting using thirty-two different shades of blue and proudly asked for their identification as separate colors. He had discovered the vast range possible in his color-mixing experiment. Inability to differentiate between light and shade, intensities and tints of colors (which amounts to an inability to see) is due to lack of training (or in some cases to color blindness). Children who are provided with mixing trays in their art classes and encouraged to experiment with colors rarely lack sensitivity in this area.

A basic aspect of color is its identity, its *hue* or its name, such as red or yellow.* When a color is bright and intense, it is further identified as being *saturated* or *full*. Mixed with black, the color is *grayed* or *muted*. Mixed with white, the color lightens in value and is called a *tint*. The gray or tint quality is often referred to as the color's *value*, or the amount of white or black it contains.

Chromatic colors are the full range of hues and are divided into *primary* colors (red, yellow, blue); *secondary colors* (green, purple, orange); and *tertiary* colors (the many different browns). Primary and secondary colors are divided into *complementary* and *analogous* colors. Complementary colors are two opposing hues, such as red and green, yellow and purple, or blue and orange. Analogous colors are closely related hues which have a common color element. In orange, red-orange, and red, the common element is red. The analogous colors to blue are blue-green and blue-purple.

Achromatic (colorless) colors are those comprising the range from white through intermediate grays to black. Grays can also be made by combining complementary colors in certain amounts.

Colors are often described as *warm* and *cold*, with reds comprising the warm colors and blues comprising the cold colors. This is a relative evaluation, however, for a "cold" blue can be surrounded by reds of varying shades and this proximity will cause the blue to appear warm.

---

* There is a certain amount of confusion among experts in color definition. Webster defines *hue* as a synonym of *color*, although hue may refer to the quality of brightness and intensity of a color, and *World Book Encyclopedia Dictionary* (Field Enterprises, 1965) refers to *hue* as "that property of a color by which it can be distinguished from grays of equal brightness." The important thing is to know generally what distinctions are referred to and to be aware of the great range and variation possible.

The important thing for the public to know is not the details of color theory, but rather that the artist is deeply concerned with color relations, with choosing, mixing, blending, and juxtaposing until he gets the right shades, saturations, tints, and grays. When colors appear to clash and shock, the artist has probably created this effect intentionally. By examining a given illustration and text, one can usually discover the reason for such effects.

The potential of color is rarely exploited to the fullest in illustrations. Color is used solely as a conventional page filler much of the time, rather than as an inherent part of the arrangement. This limited use of color is in part due to an uneasy feeling among educators that too much color overstimulates children and tends to confuse their perception. Consequently color has often been used in the manner of the child's coloring book, with an outline of black filled in with flat color. In other illustrations the color is merely window dressing, included to attract attention but not really essential to the illustration's quality. In fact, in some cases color is allowed to obscure sensitive line work.

Brian Wildsmith, Yutaka Sugita, and Suekichi Akaba are talented artist-illustrators who utilize the potential of color in their pictures. In *The Lion and the Rat* (1963), Wildsmith demonstrates a bold and inventive use of color. In other artists' colored illustrations, one can often imagine the color taken out and the picture remaining essentially the same. This is not possible with Wildsmith. He constructs the entire form of an animal or object with varying colors. These colors are not always related to the natural object, but have been added simply because that is what an artist does when he is interested in color as an art element. The different hues become Wildsmith's way of enhancing form and of suggesting the animation of nature. There is a blue rat who seems to quiver with consciousness because of the color assigned to him, as well as the textural qualities of the detail. In *Brian Wildsmith's ABC* (1963), one finds a white-and lavender-shaded yak, and in *Brian Wildsmith's Birds* (1967), a page of penguins which vibrates with pinks, blues, yellows, and oranges, besides the more conventional black and white.

Sugita, in *Have You Seen My Mother?* (1969), uses textured, vibrant ground colors and large, intensely colored shapes, yet his images remain intact with a sense of wholeness. This is difficult to achieve with such intense colors. On one page the shape of a ball is made up of raw magenta, orange, and purple sections, yet we see it as a whole, not as sections of various colors. On another page a camel is outlined with a quavery border while brilliant color is used for eye detail; yet against the stunning ground of yellows, we see that double page as a huge purplish camel.

Akaba has an intensely personal style, as seen in *Suho and the White Horse* (1969). The biggest portion of his visual statement is made by the subtly changing color grounds. He uses long horizontal areas of moody background colors—softly changing browns, red-purples, grayed tints of orange and purple, and blues—which create a sense of endless space. He draws objects (often with line in a shade of the colors he has already employed in the backgrounds) which have the hieroglyphic feeling of cave paintings.

Line

Book illustrations are most frequently developed as drawings with line. Since drawings are cheaper to reproduce than color illustrations, printing costs are undoubtedly a major factor here. Also, black-on-white drawing is a traditional mode of graphic illustration.

The line illustration is deceptive. Variations in line are not immediately evident because we are accustomed to think of line only as an outline of an object. But in the hands of a competent artist, line can be suggestive of color and can build shape and texture. A line can be wide, thin, broken, continuous, spontaneous, controlled, tight, feathery, jagged, or meandering. Simply by its style, a line can suggest mood and feeling. It can suggest movement more easily than any other art element, and many lines used together can suggest volume or form.

Margot Zemach uses line in *The Judge* (1969) both as outline and detail.

Zemach *The Judge*

She suggests architecture and interiors without detracting from the main characters—characters with frilly costuming and a mythical beast with textured horns, fur, feathers, and claws. A pale line wallpaper pattern is suggested casually (here and there rather than in continuous stripes), and since it is of light value, it never intrudes visually into the foreground lines. All Zemach's objects in this book have been so well studied and well understood that she can treat different things with different kinds of line: short curved twists of line develop the judge's wig; spare, carefully spaced straight lines suggest windows and door frames; lumpy uneven lines are used for the prisoners' and guards' clothing; while twisty continuous lines are used for elegant feminine frills. The space between and around objects provides air frames which further emphasize the line.

In *Andy Says . . . Bonjour!* (1954), the illustrator, Chris Jenkyns, meticulously uses line to report and to detail hundreds of images. He distorts the size relationships of objects to accommodate distance and intricacy of architectural and human form. His deceptively sketchy style conceals Jenkyns' intent to depict a specific kind of environment. This loose-appearing technique is sometimes neglected or dismissed casually by a hasty observer. But what appears to him as merely "sketchy" becomes, under careful examination, a line technique in which many lines are organized in varied directions to produce specific effects. The sense of vitality and humor in his line is seen in the citizens and tourists in front of Notre Dame Cathedral and in the fishing scenes. He also develops the single figures with care, being sensitive to the personalities and making them stand out by showing them as portraits against a white ground.

Blair Lent uses line in *Tikki Tikki Tembo* (1968) in another way: free, irregular lines define the objects in nature and have a watery quality, as if spreading and soaking into wet paper surfaces. For contrast the artist uses clean, precise lines for stairs, windows, Chinese pagodas, and so on.

Woodcuts and linoleum blocks are linear in nature. All parts of the wood or linoleum which should not leave an impression on the paper are cut away, and the remaining surface is inked for printing. Color may be used in block printing, but the print's strength is usually due to the light and dark contrast between the cut and uncut areas, and to the uneven textural effect achieved in the printing process. Antonio Frasconi's illustrations, discussed in the next chapter, are magnificent examples.

Other printmaking techniques are etching, lithography, and serigraphy—all extensions of drawing or linear techniques.

Shape

Since Cézanne's time, we have seen the Cubists and others stress the shape of symbols in their compositions. Sculptors are concerned with the relationships of shapes; in Alexander Calder's mobiles we see shapes hanging in space. The artist is very much aware of the single and combined shapes which he arranges in his picture, just as he is aware of color and line.

Jan Balet uses a simple black outline for object-shapes in *Joanjo* (1967), then masses and overlaps these shapes and decorates them brilliantly. His figures are static doll-like shapes. The feeling of movement is produced by tilting them, filling the page with strong diagonals. These doll-like characters are grouped so that black-framed heads curve at the top of the mass, and a collection of bare feet and shoes finishes the bottom. In between the round heads and bare feet is a potpourri of stunning decoration. The characters are like a collection of dolls from the same manufacturer, all dressed by a designer who owns an endless assortment of fabric samples.

Quite a different way of dealing with shapes can be seen in Laurence's book *A Village in Normandy* (1968). The artist uses no contour lines, and the shapes are so transparent and amorphous-seeming that only their mass creates separate and overlapping relationships. A page showing a postman and his bicycle reflected in a pond illustrates this technique. The artist's understanding of shapes, whether of chickens, cows, barns, trees, or men, permits extreme simplicity and allows her to enrich with grayed line the surface minutiae of these forms. It also permits the creation of objects in miniature, as seen at the tops of pages.

Michael Foreman uses torn paper shapes along with textured paint-over-paint landscapes in *The Two Giants* (1967). The characters look as if they had been torn out of corrugated paper and detailed with black ink. Foreman's arrangement of these shapes is free and uninhibited and creates a bold, casual concept. Eleonore Schmid's shapes in *Fenny, the Desert Fox* (1970) are in close color values and subtly modeled with short delicate lines to build mass and textural interest.

From the free-form imaginative shape to the rigidly geometric and precise shape, one will discover that shapes can suggest awkwardness, delicacy and grace, complexity, precision, boldness, stillness.

Texture
Texture is the surface characteristic of materials, as in wood, stone, grass, feathers, hair. Some artists are much involved with texture, while others may ignore it completely. It would seem that those who fall into the realist category would be the ones most preoccupied with texture, their drawings communicating the quality of materials. But the representation of the surface characteristics of materials is not always limited to realistic art. Many abstract and nonobjective artists have used contrasting surface qualities to add interest to the picture plane. Occasionally an artist develops a style which suggests an involvement with varied surface qualities in all his canvases. Van Gogh is an example. The surface treatment accomplished by his brush technique is intrinsic to the artist's expression and has become his trademark. Writing of his attempt to resolve the problem of depth of color in a manner which would suggest the firmness and strength of soil, Van Gogh said that he began with a brush, which he discarded, and then "pressed roots and trunks out of the tube and modeled them a little with my knife. There, now they stand in it, grow out of it, and have firmly taken root."[6]

38

Laurence *A Village in Normandy*

In *Bruno Munari's ABC* (1960), the artist expresses the very essence of the apple, lemon, orange, onion, pear, peanut, and walnut. He simplifies the shapes and then sensitively paints the distinguishing surface characteristic of each one. Each food form is also developed so that it has a roundness of its own and does not rely on a relative ground color or shadow outside of its own shape for the added dimension.

Particularly in his treatment of forest greenery, Bernard Waber in *A Firefly Named Torchy* (1970) emphasizes texture. Tree trunks, grasses, and foliage become fuzzy, free-form shapes and textured blots, blobs, dots, and streaks. They sparkle, dance, move with speed over the entire picture plane, explode, and make our eye move quickly in many directions. The textural effect helps sustain visual interest and excitement.

Alois Carigiet shows various textural surfaces in *The Pear Tree, the Birch Tree and the Barberry Bush* (1967). Soft grayed watercolor is used for such large areas as ground and sky, in details of bark and clothing, and as sketching line. The "little house" on the first page is defined by a wash of gray with darker grays used as line for basement stones, roof shingles, window shutters, and variations on the exterior walls.

In *Mr. Gumpy's Outing* (1970), John Burningham boldly surfaces his color areas with either changing color qualities or line, and achieves a textural movement on the picture plane that continually engages the eye. He has a variety of techniques with which he agitates the surfaces of his illustrations: for example, he uses lines of different shades to indicate curls on the sheep and feathers on the hens.

Composition

Composition is the manner in which elements of art are arranged in a picture. Composing a picture involves such considerations as balance, harmony, contrast, unity, proportion, symmetry, rhythm, movement. There are many overlapping relationships. Balance, for example, is concerned with proportions, harmony, unity, and symmetry. It would be difficult to establish exact rules for these qualities. The only thing that can be stated is that one senses a perfect synthesis in a work of merit, and one senses the neglect or absence of compositional elements in a mediocre work.

An individual's response to elements of proportion, balance, and harmony is often rooted in tradition. For example, the Western world has had, until recently, little tolerance for the void or the asymmetric in design. The acceptance of negative space is of comparatively recent origin in our culture. In the Orient, however, space is used as part of the architectural arrangement, and the oriental home and garden demonstrate a totally different sense of aesthetics connected with space. Similarly, the close color harmonies and highly patterned designs of the Near Eastern cultures seem strange to many Americans.

The use of space in the sense of breaking up a limited area with forms is a separate aesthetic phenomenon. This space, in the case of the illustration, is the limited picture plane. It is within this space that the artist composes his elements. The mood of his picture depends very largely on the sparseness or intricacy of his arrangement. Many small forms create a feeling of busyness. The feeling is altered by the shape of the forms, whether clean-edged and geometric or free-form and haptic.* But the quantity of space surrounding the shapes, and the quality of this space, is of importance to the synthesis of the picture.

Jacqueline Gachet's illustrations are beautifully ordered within rectangular and square picture planes. In *The Ladybug* (1970) clean-edged shapes of people, trees, architecture, and interiors are arranged so that every area of her plane has a feeling of deliberate organization. Objects are translated into geometric shapes and arranged against a ground which has also been divided into clean-edged shapes. There is a completeness (almost an aesthetic smugness) in each well-built page. In the first illustration the child's blue sweater and brown pants blend into the blue ground, allowing the light areas of his head and arms to con-

---

* *Haptic* refers to art expression that reflects highly subjective emotional and kinaesthetic qualities of organization, in contrast to art expression that is controlled and intellectualized. (See *haptic* in *Creative and Mental Growth* by Viktor Lowenfeld and W. L. Brittain [Macmillan, 1970].)

Foreman *The Two Giants*

nect the bright patterning of soldiers and towers at the top of the page with the bright arrangement of soldiers and cannon at the bottom. In the decorated areas Gachet often uses flat patterns of the same hue as the ground color on which they are placed, but of lighter or changed value, so that they stay within the shape edge and do not become dominant as decoration.

On one of her most successful pages, soldiers are marching toward a big gray building. The vertical edges of the buildings change from building edges as they move down the page to become the edges of three large soldier-hats. The buildings, the hats, and the men's shoulders and backs thus form a tight protective frame, enclosing a small gem-like delineation of marching soldiers.

Remy Charlip also consistently concerns himself with space and arrangement. In *The Dead Bird* (1958) the mood is created by a discreet placement of extremely simple objects on large, unmoving areas of close-harmonied colors. The same objects (trees in a forest, children, a dead bird) are seen repeatedly through-

Charlip *A Day of Summer*

42

out the book, but from radically different "camera angles." Some views are close-ups, as in the double page of four large children finding the small, still bird. This view is then enlarged as though the artist had used a telescopic lens in his perception. In fact, some of the views become so enlarged that we see only a portion of the children's heads.

In Charlip's *A Day of Summer* (1960) an insect-sized, diminutive girl is placed on a textured green ground, watching enormous clouds in the bright, raw-blue sky. Size contrast is also impressive when the artist places a larger-than-life circle of peaches in the foreground and a tiny woman on the horizon hanging clothes.

The Artist's Personal View

Our search for criteria has revealed several points. First, one must recognize that illustrations belong to the realm of visual art and are appropriately judged by criteria derived from the fine arts. Then the illustration is analyzed to determine which elements of art seem to carry the burden of the artist's statement —color, line, shape, texture, or composition. Once this preference has been identified, the art elements are examined for the specific way in which they have been used. If the artist's statement is made with line, for example, one examines this line for variety, expressiveness, simplicity, or other dynamic qualities.

The closer the scrutiny, the more rewarding the results will be. One discovers that the illustration which seemed to be brightly colored is in reality only strong in light and dark contrasts. Or, what seemed to be an interest in color is in reality black brush drawing on different-colored background papers. Or it is seen that the sense of movement is achieved by having all lines point in the same direction, the focal point lying outside the picture space. The extent of discovery depends upon the degree of commitment to this kind of visual analysis. One begins to *see*, literally, what the artist can do with visual elements, within the limitations of space.*

The mediocre artist repeats the same stereotypes in every book, regardless of the content or mood required. The skilled artist-illustrator demonstrates his awareness of the variety of ways each element may be used, as well as the possibilities of combining one with another. The mediocre artist, in repeating his formula in book after book, indicates that he either is not aware of these varied possibilities, or else considers it unimportant to become involved. In either case, unwilling or unable, the result is predictably inferior to that work which shows respect for the book form, the art elements, and the viewer.

Personal interpretation in the visual arts is a kind of editorializing, a deliberate emphasis or exaggeration in treatment. For example, many contempo-

---

*S. I. Hayakawa feels that the majority of us are visually "object-minded" and not "relation-minded." To remedy this, he suggests that something of the quality of a child's delight in playing with colors and shapes has to be restored to us before we can learn to see again, "before we unlearn the terms in which we ordinarily see." (Introduction to Gyorgy Kepes' *Language of Vision*, Paul Theobald, Chicago, 1945.)

Newberry *Pandora*

Frasconi *The House That Jack Built*

Sokol *Cats, Cats, Cats, Cats, Cats*

Rand *I Know a Lot of Things*

Birnbaum *Green Eyes*

Eichenberg *Ape in a Cape*

Jenkyns *Andy Says . . . Bonjour!*

Chermayeff *Peter Pumpkin*

rary illustrators have interpreted the city in various ways. Ludwig Bemelmans gives a dimension of gaiety and movement to the metropolis. He portrays a large scene, and adds infinite minutiae, usually people of many types decorated with bold and gay detail. In contrast, Bernard Waber depicts old tenement architecture with strong, slashing lines in *Rich Cat, Poor Cat* (1963), and Garth Williams makes a cynical commentary on the impersonal and gloomy urban dweller in *The Three Little Animals* (1956). With similar variations in emphasis, the inscrutable personality of the cat is perceived and expressed by artists Sokol, Jenkyns, Rand, Newberry, Frasconi, Chermayeff, Eichenberg, and Birnbaum.

It is a natural function of the artist to interpret. He selects from the elements of art those which will assist his interpretation and screens out those which will detract. But basic to the interpretation is the artist's own feeling about the objects or scenes being portrayed. When we recognize the painting as a visible document of an artist's feeling about something, we add another dimension to our picture viewing. We stop insisting that the picture reflect our feelings about the city, for example, and instead we try to understand someone else's perception. We may not feel lonely ourselves in a city, but since we know what loneliness is, we ought to sense that quality when it is presented by an artist. Using a rural and wooded setting, Remy Charlip successfully conveys a sense of sadness and loneliness in *The Dead Bird* (1958).

A work of art which is genuinely expressive is a highly personal and unique phenomenon. No two artists bring an identical set of emotions, attitudes, and experiences to bear on picture making. This personal attitude is the background from which the artist interprets and selects his elements. When one says that an artist really "has something to say," one usually refers to the quality of synthesis that is felt in his painting. Creating this synthesis is a disciplined sensory activity. It is only by looking at the picture with similar discipline that the critic can receive the communication intended. When this kind of reception becomes intuitive, one perceives a new work of art much as one does a new friend, by recognizing the differences, noting them, and finding satisfaction in having acquired something new, novel, and stimulating.

4

Outstanding Contemporary Illustrators

I<small>N THE LAST</small> two or three decades, an increasing number of artists of national and international reputation have been commissioned to illustrate children's books. Artists mentioned in this chapter and the preceding one have been connected with the mainstream of contemporary graphics and painting, and some have studied under major artists and teachers at the Art Students League, Pratt Institute, Cooper Union, the École des Beaux-Arts, and other institutions. Some are easel painters who have exhibited in the principal American galleries and museums.

Illustrations by some of these artists are presented here. These artists are standard-bearers in children's literature, illustrators who have used the book as an art form and endowed the page with the same aesthetic qualities they incorporate in an easel painting or other graphic work. They have personal and unique styles. They represent the contemporary idiom, utilizing the elements of art to express a variety of ideas in many ways. They interpret the text with directness and sincerity.

The aim of this chapter is to focus attention on some of this outstanding work and at the same time to demonstrate a mode of inquiry and criticism which can be used in examining the artwork in other picture books. Dozens of additional books by the illustrators mentioned here, and by many other artists, could be studied for their superior craftsmanship and unique styles.*

Ludwig Bemelmans (1898–1962)
Ludwig Bemelmans was born in the Tyrol, in Austria, and attended schools

---

* Photographic picture books have been purposely excluded because, generally speaking, their quality has not been high. However, photography may have a greater potential than has yet been demonstrated in books for the very young.

in Regensburg and Rothenburg, Bavaria. He was a resident of Paris off and on throughout his life, as well as of New York City.

Bemelmans' style is based on a strong sense of design and an ability to suggest movement. In *Madeline* (1939) he uses the "twelve little girls" as page patterns. Wherever the twelve are placed, they are so arranged that the grouping of twelve similar shapes of capes, round hats, and thin legs forms a design on the page. His designer skills are evident also in the large full-page paintings in which he depicts monumental buildings, the panorama of a park, the zoo—all with the same humorous, free, and highly personal style.

A Bemelmans trademark is his ease in handling intricate architectural detail such as the facade of Notre Dame in Paris. He washes a color over and beyond the area in which he plans to place a building. The area of the wash is not specifically limited to or related to the structure of the building. He uses the same technique for the delineation of trees, and for the large white decorative urns in the park. This manner is very like that of the Dufy brothers in technique as well as in mood. The effect is gay and energetic, with an animated sense of design and pattern. His black-and-white pages are often audacious in their movement, as in the extreme acute angle used for Miss Clavel to run "fast and faster."

In *Madeline's Rescue* (1953) Bemelmans continues in the same decorative manner, but the groupings of the twelve little girls are more variously handled. He utilizes the wide-brimmed hats, capes, and thin legs occasionally as one large shape; on one page all twelve little girls become a single blue shape, which is detailed not with his usual black line but with smaller shapes—twelve white collars, gloves, stockings, oval faces, and yellow hats. This kind of tightly knit design of smaller shapes and colors within a larger shape is illustrative of Bemelmans' awareness of design and his talent for reducing many complicated objects to a cohesive and decorative whole.

Sometimes Bemelmans forsakes elaborate background detail in favor of a solid-color ground wash. In *Madeline in London* (1961) a double-page spread contains brilliantly colored birds, the girls' twelve yellow capes, and the guards' vermilion capes and white hats against a dull green ground color. On other pages (and this is more customary for Bemelmans) he fills the page from bottom to top with people, buildings, trees, fences, statues—everything his eye has recorded. As in other books, he reduces human forms into design patterns and still retains a feeling of movement. Sometimes this is accomplished by assigning the feeling of movement not only to one individual but to a whole crowd of people, who seem to move together as a river, flowing out from an urban background and becoming quite specific in the foreground.

Few artists have portrayed contemporary humanity as perceptively and sympathetically as Bemelmans, or with such pleasing spontaneity.

Marcia Brown (1918–   )
Marcia Brown studied at the Woodstock School of Painting under Judson Smith; at the New York School for Social Research under Yasui Kuniyoshi,

48

Brown *Cinderella*

49

Stuart Davis, and Louis Shankar; at the Art Students League under Julian Levi; and at the Columbia University Graduate School of Philosophy. She is an author, illustrator, librarian, painter, teacher of puppetry, and graphic artist.

Marcia Brown is talented, versatile, and eclectic in her personal aesthetics. She is an experimentalist, even changing her direction and manner of working within a single book. Sometimes she orders and controls her object-forms meticulously and carefully; at other times a great abandonment characterizes her sketches and page design. Regardless of mode, however, her work is highly imaginative and spirited.

In *Henry—Fisherman* (1949) Brown frankly decorates the surface of the pages with solid, poster-like shapes, and uses line only for intricate detail. The pages reveal the great variety of surface treatments possible on flat areas of color: squares, dots, stripes, lines, and the infinite variation of each of these as they are combined, reduced, enlarged, juxtaposed. There is a vigorous market scene viewed behind a large tree which goes out of the top of the page and whose leaves at the top form part of the picture's limits. The scene itself is a decorative organization of discrete black and white shapes on a red ground color, arranged to give the illusion of about two dozen people and their assorted wares. This is a consistently controlled manner of working. She flattens the picture plane and decorates it with solid-color areas and clean-edged patterning. The style is reminiscent of Stuart Davis, under whom Marcia Brown studied.

One of Brown's most interesting and personal styles was developed in *Puss-in-Boots* (1952). Here she suggests the forms of objects in shaded gray areas and uses a thin, delicate contour line to detail and to complete the object. Some of the forms are indeterminate and incomplete, but the feeling and illusion are convincing. The line does not always function as contour, but sometimes suggests texture, with the light and dark contrasts of shaded grays and pinks and yellows carrying the burden of building the object-forms. One of the most convincing illusions Brown develops in this book is the quality of lacy and frilly fabrics. She uses a delicate, wavy, curled line to build this illusion, especially successful in her treatment of the king's daughter.

The artist uses line in this manner in *Cinderella* (1954) and uses the same technique of suggesting form with neutral grays. She uses minimal line and color in her first portrait of Cinderella, a meticulous handling of technique to create a mood of fragile, sentimental, other-worldly femininity. This wistful mood is maintained throughout, to the last delicately drawn, fairy-like illusion of Cinderella and the fairy godmother. Brown seems to be very comfortable and spontaneous in this style. Her technique seems to be the result of a synthesis of means and ends. The feeling she initially had for the story is convincingly translated into the sensitive line, which delicately and rhythmically expresses this feeling on the picture page.

Woodcuts are used for the fable *Once a Mouse* (1961). For the most part, silhouettes of forms of one color and textural quality are superimposed on another block of a different color. The pages are often strongly designed as well

Fischer *The Birthday*

as highly patterned. The overall light and dark contrasts produce vitality and a sense of movement, although the simple masses representing the trees and people tend to quiet the movement, making sensitively balanced compositions.

Hans Fischer (1909–1958)

Hans Fischer was a Swiss artist who studied at the École des Beaux-Arts in Paris, as well as at the Arts Décoratifs in Geneva under Paul Klee. In addition to his work as an illustrator, he was an easel painter, graphic artist (etchings and lithographs), mural and poster painter, and stage designer.

Hans Fischer, or "Fis," as he signs his paintings and graphics, is expert with line. He can use line simply to contour forms or playfully and fancifully as decoration, or he can build mood and shadows by combining lines in mass. In *The Traveling Musicians* (1955) he exhibits the full scope of his graphic talents.

François *Roland*

He sometimes delineates forms by a contour line which, in its simplicity, is deceptively modest. Or his line may meander, wiggle, or curve as he plays with the linear possibilities suggested by the scene. He also uses line as pattern and decoration, with circles, spirals, stripes, squares, checks, and many other motifs combined with much the same feeling of humor that Paul Klee captured in his art. He further uses a crosshatched massing of lines as grain and texture, or as shading to develop forms from light to dark. This latter technique serves the purpose of either building form or creating a dark, gloomy, night mood.

In *Pitschi* (1953) Fischer's line becomes more fanciful. Attention is given to a variety of objects, so that some pages become extremely full graphic statements. There is a riot of movement in the last double-page drawing of the garden. One must examine the page inch by inch in order to see all the plants and animals. The quality of the line remains delightfully uninhibited, even with the burden of depicting such a tremendous variety of materials. (Note, for example, the differentiated flower forms.) There are two dark, crosshatched pictures in *Pitschi*. One is foreboding and fearsome, depicting a wolf, a kitten, owls, and bats; the other is of a house in the woods, drawn to create a dark and dramatic feeling. This style contrasts with his light, delicate, fanciful sketches.

Fischer follows the same manner of picture-making in *The Birthday* (1954); but he uses a sketchier style in his version of *Puss-in-Boots* (1959). His line is wider and softer, different from the crisp black line we have been examining. There is vitality as well as a capacity to capture the feeling of movement inherent in the object he is defining. Some of the light-colored lines are, however, not altogether successful in carrying their share of the design burden of the page.

André François (1915–   )

André François was born in Rumania, but attended the École des Beaux-Arts in Paris, and Cassandre's School of Fine Arts. He is a theater set designer, advertising artist, and illustrator.

François's art truly has a sense of gaiety. His line covers the page in what Grosz might have characterized as the "pure joy of decorative creation." He deliberately flattens all the forms and systematically covers the entire surface with pattern. His use of sumptuous floral and geometric forms as decoration is suggestive of the Byzantine mode of richly patterned surfaces.

In *Roland* (1958) François uses flat areas of ochre, blue, black, and white to make a large design, and the same range of colors for the detailed decoration. He demonstrates his designer skills by taking a scene which requires the dimension of depth (a room interior or a landscape), flattening all the forms within the dimension, and proceeding to decorate the surfaces. Each picture gives one the feeling that everything in it is dangling from invisible strings on one vertical plane. Perspective is suggested by receding diagonal lines and by the decreasing sizes of floors, windows, desks, and rugs in the interior scenes, and by buildings, sidewalks, lampposts, and the placement of people of different sizes in the exterior scenes. François orders a large visual image into a limited picture space, and

Frasconi *The House That Jack Built*

Kepes *Beasts from a Brush*

once his objects are in place, he decorates with stripes, dots, speckles, scratches, stipples, flowers, and many line variations. If one starts at the bottom of the page and conscientiously moves one's line of vision to the top, one begins to see the vast panorama. On one page, an especially effective design has buildings framing the top and right-hand side of the picture, creating an unusual, asymmetrical sense of balance. A large urban square (on another page) is treated in similar fashion, with diminishing sizes assigned to the flat, yet receding, figures at the top of the picture. The figures are simplified forms, serving as silhouette patterns on the snow. The meandering ochre lines of the bicycle tracks further unify an ingeniously designed page. The final impression from *Roland* is of a joyful, puppet-like, static construction.

François works in a completely linear style (very like that of George Grosz) in *Little Boy Brown* (1949). Thin black lines carry the entire burden of the pictorial statement, with the brown wash simply being there, serving no special design function. Subtle expressions of animation are suggested on the enlarged heads of the figures. Here, as in *Roland*, François demonstrates his ability to translate and reduce panoramic urban vistas to small, simplified, and magnificently detailed forms. His thin broken line transforms the city into decoration. His page layouts and handling of symmetry add to the gleeful quality of the pages, with miniature objects placed off-center. Two illustrations depicting a bus reveal the ease and whimsy with which François can handle difficult perspective views. In one, the viewer looks directly into the passengers' faces; in the other, the rear of the bus is cut away figuratively, and the viewer sees the backs of the seats in the last row.

Antonio Frasconi (1919–   )

Antonio Frasconi was born in Montevideo, Uruguay, and attended the Circulo des Bellas Artes, Montevideo. He later studied with Kuniyoshi at the Art Students League. Frasconi received the Guggenheim Memorial Foundation's Inter-American Fellowship to illustrate the poetry of Walt Whitman and García Lorca, and he has had numerous other awards and honors. He is a woodcut artist, lithographer, teacher, and illustrator; his work has been widely exhibited.

Frasconi's pages need to be looked at with directness. One must discard preconceived notions about how objects "should" be portrayed and substitute instead the freshest approach possible. As one uses a fresher vision, the expressiveness and uniqueness of his artistry become apparent. Frasconi saturates every object with expressive vigor. All the elements of art are synthesized to achieve this feeling of intensity—superior craftsmanship and technique, a selective use of color, a strong sense of design, and an instinctive feeling for emphasis which he achieves by distortion and exaggeration.

In *See and Say* (1955) this quality is evident in every woodcut in the book. Textures of materials have been simulated with variety and expertness, and are inseparable from the outline of the objects. They appear to have been developed simultaneously. The feathered fatness of the chicken, the ordered tile roofs of houses, the abstracted engineer-like feeling of the bridge structure, the power and push of the sea, the soft quilt-like fullness of the bed, the worn-ness of the shoes—all these are unified in feeling.

The House That Jack Built (1958) is more powerful in its impact because here Frasconi uses full pages to treat single visual concepts. He reduces his ideas to an essence of form and texture, as in illustrations of the potent rat, the self-satisfied cat, the worried cow, the vital maid in motion, and the arrogant rooster.

Although nonobjective art, as such, has rarely been used in the picture book, sometimes the artist's style emphasizes the "how" in the art elements much more than the "what" that he is portraying. When this happens, one responds to the "how" also. When Frasconi's forms and techniques carry expressive power, one responds to these forms, noting the expressive quality first and later noting the objects depicted. The title page in *The Snow and the Sun* (1961) is illustrative of this vitality, suggesting the tug and movement of nature's forces. On another page, lines, directions, color contrasts, and surface agitation contribute to the success of a double page in which wind, sun, and snow are symbolized and seem felt by the woman in distress. An example of the way Frasconi uses objects as design forms, to carry expressive qualities, is the black, wooden fence structure which encloses a cow. A highly personalized portrait of a man looking straight out of the picture at the viewer is suggestive of some of the woodcuts of the German Expressionists.

Juliet Kepes (1919–   )

Juliet Kepes was born in England and attended Askes Hotcham in London, the Brighton School of Art, and later the Chicago School of Design. She is an easel

56

painter, sculptor, and mural and screen painter, as well as an illustrator.

Juliet Kepes designs pages with a sensitive feeling for balance. Her line is graceful and fluid. Sometimes she eliminates details, relying completely on the movement and ease of her line. At other times she uses detail for emphasis and decoration. Her pages have an oriental quality with asymmetrical balance and a feeling of space, restraint, and quiet.

Beasts from a Brush (1955) is consistently linear. Kepes designs graceful, mostly curvilinear, animals, and although they are drawn with utmost precision, still they convey the illusion of spontaneity. She plans her page space with concern for the whole effect as well as for the particulars of her simply and elegantly stated animals and birds. She accomplishes this by judicious balance and the use of white ground areas with contrasting detail.

In *Two Little Birds and Three* (1960) Kepes creates beautiful page designs with gray washes, soft black foliage, pink flower details, white soft-edged bird

forms (as of torn paper), and delicate, thin, black-and-white line for detail. There is a most gentle and tender feeling achieved by this technique, a sense of frailty which adds to the quiet, soft quality of the pages.

In *Lady Bird, Quickly* (1964) Kepes introduces her book with endpapers of magenta ladybug shapes on a brilliant blue ground. The color combinations are often unusual: greens and purples, oranges and pinks, two raw greens. The pages are arranged with large areas acting as foils for small, delicate bug details. Her line and pattern are ingeniously employed, and occasionally she adds soft suggestions of textures for further surface interest.

Leo Lionni (1910–   )

Leo Lionni was born in Amsterdam, received his Ph.D. in economics from the University of Genoa, and studied painting in Europe. He has been a painter, architect, designer, teacher, mosaic artist, graphics artist, art director for *Fortune* magazine, design consultant for many American and foreign corporations, and recipient of numerous awards and honors. He has exhibited widely and is one of the most versatile book illustrators.

Lionni's main involvement in illustration seems to be with the surface appearance of forms and with the arrangement of these textured forms on the picture page.

In *Inch by Inch* (1960) he varies nature's surfaces and shapes, and carefully assigns a specific surface color and texture to each blade of grass, leaf, tree trunk, bird, flower—to everything he uses in his pictures. The only object that is immune to this treatment is the inchworm, which remains a solid color without texture. Since the inchworm is very small, this contrast enables one to find him, usually after a search. Some of the surface treatment is based on the natural object, while other surfaces borrow from sources outside nature. For example, the robin's texture is quite frankly a textile design pattern which has been most successfully and ingeniously appropriated. Each page has high visual interest, not only because of the clean-edged, cut-out look and consistent treatment of the objects, but also because of the page layouts. His designs are dramatic, as in one illustration of a heron, with legs zipping out of the page with a strong vertical and head swinging back into the page at the right. His color sense adds to the vivid quality of the book.

Lionni's preoccupation with the surface qualities of forms comes very close to the nonobjective in *Swimmy* (1963). He seems interested in the textures he invents for their own sake, rather than their relationship to any real object. If it were not for the occasional fish stereotype which he uses on the title page, the forms, shapes, sizes, and colors would have no particular underwater connotation. The page would be suggestive of nature, but not of specific areas of nature; rather, nature in a generic sense in contrast to the man-made world. Every page is an experiment in surface texturing: sponge in paint, paint dripped, brayer rolling, doily painting, and so on.* Young children are familiar with these experimental techniques since *gadget painting* is part of their art curriculum. Part of the great charm of this book to children lies in their own interest in surface explorations. Lionni has engaged in some of these same gadget painting experiments, but always with the controlled talent of a mature artist.

In contrast to the richly diversified surface treatments in *Swimmy,* Lionni's simple fish stereotype is stamped repeatedly, with no color variation, over the entire picture page. The result is somewhat monotonous. Another fish, a large black tuna, is diversified in textural treatment and is more successful visually. Interest is also maintained on a page with a colorfully surfaced lobster. Sometimes his sense of page design suffers because of his involvement with special effects, as in his preoccupation with the imprint made by a paper doily.

Alexander and the Wind-Up Mouse (1969) sustains visual interest, but it is also a little too stagy. Lionni uses all his gifts (and he has an abundance) but this becomes more than the book needs. *Frederick* (1967) is more sensitive throughout because it maintains the mood suggested at the beginning; it is a synthesis from cover to cover, the same song. Lionni arranges, in collage fashion, shape assortments of mice and rocks in a soft, quiet range of grays. The varied shapes reside so comfortably within the picture plane that Lionni makes his visual task seem effortless. All the shapes, except the mice, have clean edges and textured interiors. The illusion of furriness on the mice is created by the torn edges of the dark gray paper used for their bodies. This furriness contrasts simply with the clean edges of their ears, legs, and tails.

Nicholas Mordvinoff (1911–   )

Nicholas Mordvinoff was born in Leningrad. He attended the University of Paris and is an easel painter, sculptor, graphic artist, and illustrator.

Mordvinoff is a bold, expressive draftsman and uses his linear technique in various ways. At times his line is thin and economical and merely suggests the object. At other times this same thin line is used to develop the object in minute and revealing detail. Then again the line becomes thick, is more modified in tone, and is used to suggest form with lights and darks.

In *The Two Reds* (1950) Mordvinoff draws a wistful boy, Joey, and a wistful cat, Mr. Furpatto Purcatto. The boy's head, with the exception of the hair, is stated with a few simple, expressive black lines on a white ground. The hair is depicted by many scraggly red lines, as are the eyebrows. The cat is a red and white shape with no outline, but with many small lines used to give the textural illusion of fur. This is the way of the book. The characteristic quality of each article is depicted in a minimal way. Some of the objects make up a large statement, as in a double page showing a fruit vendor, his cart loaded with fruits and vegetables, the horse, Mr. Purcatto, and Joey. Some pages are portraits of a

---

*Brayer rolling is achieved by coating a cylindrical printing tool (called a *brayer* and similar to a paint roller) with paint and rolling it on paper which is placed over a textured surface of string, leaves, etc. The imprint of the textured object underneath comes through in a darker value, while the paper surface is also textured with a general uneven tone. A variation of this technique is to wrap a string around the brayer first, then dip it in paint and roll it on paper.

few objects, as of Joey and cat, drawn large and expressively. Bright red is used throughout to spot the cat and Joey's hair. Occasionally the use of red is extended, unfortunately, into too much of the picture, making it difficult to see the line. Line is Mordvinoff's forte, and it seems unwise to obscure the quality of the line by a bright spot of red color.

In *Finders Keepers* (1951) Mordvinoff extends his drawing technique, using rapid foreshortening to include more faraway objects in the picture page. His page design is an exceptional feature in this book; shapes, colors, textures, and details are expertly handled to make a synthesis. Color is used to build a scene, and not simply as a page-filler. There is a striking double page of two ochre dogs on a red road which starts very wide at the bottom left of the page and curves rapidly to the upper right, diminishing to a thin curved line over the hill. The ground areas on both sides of the red road are black shapes into which two black trees merge for a while and then leave the shape to go out of the picture page at the top. Four ochre hill shapes are placed behind the two black trees. Animal portraiture continues here as in *The Two Reds*; in this instance, the subject is a magnificently frenetic goat.

The Little Tiny Rooster (1960) is again an expressive, bold, bustling statement. At times, Mordvinoff uses large forms alone, as in the portrait of the sun: a round red shape outlined in blue and framed in irregular red and white, all on a blue ground. He also works with many forms and can handle panoramic ideas, as in a barnyard scene with many small shapes, infinitely detailed. The leaves and branches of two different trees, five different roof treatments, the silo treatment, and so on, demonstrate Mordvinoff's facility with concepts. His sense of design is displayed throughout the book, as in a tight arrangement of three cows, a rhythmic line pattern of a flock of chickens, and a page layout in which he places diagonal, strong, light-and-dark contrasts over a large double page. The book has such a feeling of energy and movement that even in the carefully crosshatched picture of hens roosting in the shadowy moonlight, we sense that the repose is illusory; come dawn, with the rooster's first crow, the crosshatched lines will fly!

Celestino Piatti (1922–   )

Celestino Piatti attended the School for Applied Arts in Zurich, Switzerland, and is widely known as an advertising and poster artist as well as an illustrator. He has exhibited his work internationally.

Piatti combines wide line with thin detailed line, includes color as a real art element on the page, richly textures and decorates the forms he uses in his illustrations, arranges them boldly on the picture page, and, with a happy synthesis of all the art elements, creates a rich sensory experience.

The Happy Owls (1964) is such an experience. Each page is treated with a noticeable alertness to design. The owls have been simplified in form, but their surface decoration of patterned feathers is anything but simple. This elaboration of a simply stated shape into a smart, colorful bit of decoration is typical of Piatti's work. Owls, barnyard fowl, a gorgeous peacock—all are colorful and

Mordvinoff *Little Tiny Rooster*

Piatti *The Happy Owls*

vivid. There is an effective spring landscape in which Piatti builds a most contemporary painting with varying colors, lines, textures, and shapes and achieves a close and complete synthesis of all these elements.

The Holy Night (1968) is another example of this style. Piatti builds large shapes and outlines them in black. Then he breaks up the interior of the shape into smaller shapes of varying sizes (often in a geometric fashion) with the same black line. His initial large shape concept is extremely simple, almost sculptural. His colors are in the dark, somber, gray and brown range, but each page uses small bits of raw color (turquoise and magenta) or white for contrast. There are noteworthy examples of detailed architectural areas and of brick walls, stone streets, garden walls, and foliage.

In *The Nock Family Circus* (1968) Piatti treats shapes without the usual heavy black outline which characterizes his style in other picture books. Shapes are sometimes contrasted in color value to the background but more often they are very close in value. This low-intensity, close-value technique creates a moody, often somber quality by its grayness. This is a more painterly and less decorator-oriented approach. The surfaces are treated with less stylization but with freer and richer paint texture. Line functions less as decoration and more in defining areas and objects. The grayed colors continue throughout the book, the larger shapes mottled with darker values of their base color. Occasionally Piatti uses a bit of raw color but not in sufficient quantity to break the quiet feeling. An illustration of the interior of a tent complements perfectly the text: "cool and dim and very quiet." The ground color and the tent canopy are defined as large grayed-green shapes. The five small people function as shapes but are kept in size and color in a subdued relationship to the mass of greens. Small spots of bright red and blue serve as beautiful accents, building a tidy, clean-edged geometry of varied shapes against larger grayed blue-greens.

Although Piatti uses a different manner of illustrating in this book, he still relates to shapes as the dominant element in his art, with notable variations in utilizing them.

Nicolas Sidjakov (1924–   )
Nicolas Sidjakov was born in Riga, Latvia. He studied painting at the École des Beaux-Arts in Paris, and is a free-lance artist, illustrator, and designer. He contributed much design work to the French postwar motion picture industry.

Sidjakov *Baboushka and the Three Kings*

Sidjakov combines the art mannerisms of long ago with a thoroughly contemporary attitude. He is a master decorator; he combines a twentieth century boldness with the decorative traditions of Byzantium and medieval stained glass.

In *The Friendly Beasts* (1957) he deliberately cuts black lines through brightly colored areas, creating geometric forms within the shapes of the simplified and stylized sheep, cows, and other objects. He uses the swirl motif repeatedly on the sheep's back and the cow's head for added decoration and for textural suggestion. He creates a decorative linear design in the angel and star forms and in the Mary and Joseph scene, where the black line stands out richly and vibrantly, contrasting with the colorful background. The mode is flat, stylized; the forms are bold, decorative, and colorful. The result is a feeling of great richness.

In *Baboushka and the Three Kings* (1960) Sidjakov works in a similar fashion but with less reliance on color. He deliberately flattens his forms and puts all the objects on the same picture plane. This is seen in a picture of Baboushka, chair, window, wooden bucket, stove, cat, and candlestick. Simultaneously, he alters the forms of the objects, reducing them to varied geometric symbols, and knitting them tightly into a handsome design. Such stylization is evident in a picture of horses and chariots, and in a picture of the three kings where each is given the appearance of a puppet or wooden doll.

There is little suggestion of movement in this formalized concept of art, since the artist's interests lie in other directions. Sidjakov works as the Byzantine artist of earlier centuries. He depersonalizes the human form, suspends movement, and symbolizes the human being statically. In doing this, the artist now has an impersonal surface which he can embellish. The vitality in this kind of art is in the design itself and in the variety of ways the artist can break up the flat color areas with geometric shapes, as well as with textures and small design details.

Sidjakov draws compact villages and buildings with line alone. In these black line drawings, he creates the illusion of architectural compactness, and at the same time adds decoration by alternating horizontally and vertically striped areas. He also has a whimsical painting of a snowstorm. It is executed on a streaked, grayed-blue ground and is more suggestive of mood than his flat, decorated pages.

Bill Sokol (1925–   )

Bill Sokol was born in Warsaw and spent his childhood in New York. He is an advertising art director, a graphic arts designer, easel painter, and illustrator.

Sokol's line is beautifully interpretative. It not only suggests the form it is building, it does so with delicacy and elegance.

Sokol uses an ingenious form on the dedication page of *A Child's Book of Dreams* (1957). He textures a bird form variously, with horizontal short strokes on the breast and alternating thin and thick lines stroked diagonally on the wings. There are two circles for eyes, an arrow shape for the beak, and two thin lines

Bemelmans *Madeline in London*

Sendak *The Moon Jumpers*

Sokol *The Emperor and the Nightingale*

for the legs, impossibly supporting the large, inverted tear-drop form of the bird. It is a simple, gentle, and whimsical concept. From here on, Sokol develops each page with feeling and with utmost care for technique and details. There are changing lines of rolling hills; ethereal, magical trees and birds; mountains of ice cream and twirling lines of sky and ground; an arrogant cat with flowers blooming at the end of his whiskers. All are examples of Sokol's fanciful and sympathetic treatment of the stuff of children's dreams.

Sokol draws cats on the endpapers and on the title page of *Cats, Cats, Cats, Cats, Cats* (1958) with the same perceptive and sensitive line. His understanding of the mannerisms and appearance of cats is exceptionally acute. He develops page after page of cat studies, either singly or in combination with interior furnishings, people, or other cats. All the graphic art shows the same range of awareness and the book jacket in particular is a beautifully interpretative bit of drawing.

In *The Emperor and the Nightingale* (1959) Sokol develops a mood at the start of the book with his endpapers. He has designed a mystical hilltop forested with blue, green, and red-brown trees, and lit by a spinning, shining sun. He later restates this hilltop in black and white and extends it to include a still higher hilltop in the left of the picture page, topped with a palace. The sun, even in black and white, is a vital spinning illusion. His line technique is different here. In *Book of Dreams* and *Cats, Cats, Cats, Cats, Cats* he uses a thin, delicate line which he varies in thickness purposely to achieve greater plasticity of form or to achieve textural effects. His line in *The Emperor and the Nightingale* is thicker, varies with spots and blotches, and is used in conjunction with gray tones. The effect is dynamic and vigorous. These spotted areas give a feeling of agitation and movement which Sokol occasionally contrasts and relieves by including his quiet, soft gray line. (These gray lines are also used to suggest distance.) This technique is used for the nightingale. The darker and more uneven lines form the wings and the gray lines gently outline the breast, making a convincing suggestion of form. The artificial nightingale is developed more elegantly, in a fanciful, abstract manner. It is profusely decorated with curves, stripes, dots, spots, spirals—all on a ground of smaller, swirling design patterns.

Taro Yashima (1908–   )

Taro Yashima was born in Japan and educated at the Imperial Art Academy of Tokyo. Later he was a student at the Art Students League. He is an easel painter and graphic artist as well as an illustrator.

Yashima's technique is romantic and sentimental. An intimate quality is communicated to the viewer. This shared intimacy is achieved through the use of light and dark areas in his picture design. These contrasts contribute a subtle quality and a poetic mood to the drawing, often a gentle, quiet mood. At the same time, the light areas can be so bathed in artificial light that there is also a resulting sense of drama. It is almost as if the viewer held a bright flashlight, flooding the diorama. Yashima creates his forms by this illusion also, as in the people and animals stated as light against dark in *The Village Tree* (1953). Two children are built completely by light and dark areas, as well as the farmer, and the child and the goat in another illustration. The forms are sometimes actually broken and the color which would normally be assigned to the object replaced by a shape of

Sokol *The Emperor and the Nightingale*

Yashima *Umbrella*

white or light color. This creates depth in the object and differentiates the specific parts that make the whole image.

In *Umbrella* (1958) he handles this technique deftly and creates a shimmering softness reminiscent of some of the Impressionists' work. The child's whimsical face and figure are delicately handled with dark and light contrasts, and an occasional sensitive line is added to delineate details such as the umbrella, the toes, or a straggle of hair. These line details are used on both the light and the dark areas and are treated with understatement and taste. They add to

67

the sentimental aura of the book. The *sgrafitto* technique* is an interesting and successful addition to the surfaces of some of the pictures. The perspective device of looking over an object in the foreground to strikingly foreshortened background objects is used effectively in the pictures of figures in the rain.

In *The Seashore Story* (1967) soft pastel colors are blended and smudged into fuzzy-edged shapes of landscape. Occasional line details appear in the large masses but are never obtrusive; one needs to search for them. Yashima's people are delineated similarly—fuzzy-edged, but with light and dark contrasts building the body structure. A giant turtle is developed in the same manner. The four large oval deep-water shapes tend to be monotonous. It seems as though Yashima might have detailed them variously or altered them in some way to add to their visual interest. The double-page spreads are, for the most part, nicely planned with the text at the bottom. Exceptions are the three double pages of figures at the beach which do not seem to be organically planned. One's eye does not carry visually from one side of the page to the other or from one figure to the other. These pages are more suggestive of the figures in an artist's sketchbook, done with no particular need for synthesis and lacking the appearance of a finished and planned arrangement of shapes.

Reiner Zimnik (1930–   )

Reiner Zimnik was born in Beuthen, Upper Silesia. He studied at the Academy of Fine Arts in Munich, Germany, where he now makes his home.

Zimnik accomplishes miracles with his agile line drawings. He suggests movement, busyness, quietness, mass, humor, flight—all in an immensely ingenious manner. In *Jonah the Fisherman* (1956) twenty-nine assorted, striding fishermen are drawn on the frontispiece. The men and their fishing rods make a delicately moving curve of repeated line patterns on the lower third of the picture page. In the next illustration Zimnik starts at the upper right-hand corner, curves a little and then makes a long graceful linear curve toward the lower left corner. This is the bank of the Seine, and there are fifty-three fishermen sitting on the bank. Their fishing rods suggest distance and also make a pattern on the remainder of the page with fifty-three variously angled lines. Zimnik brings many objects forward from a distance: ships, nets of fish, buffaloes, and a page of twenty-two tractors, the last of which recedes to a dot on the horizon.

Some of Zimnik's recurring textural delineations are seen in his clouds, sky, beards, foliage, and always in smoke—pipe smoke, car smoke, boat smoke, city and building smoke, bonfire smoke, and so forth. Sometimes he masses line to create a value contrast, as in trouser cloth differentiated from shirt fabric, or in

---

Sgrafitto is a crayon scratching technique with which children are familiar. Wax crayon is applied to the paper surface in large, solid areas. Black crayon is then applied over these colored areas, completely coating all the previously crayoned surfaces. A drawing is now scratched through the black surface with a sharp tool such as a nail. Wherever the black is removed, the colors underneath come through.

Zimnik *Jonah the Fisherman*

69

Zimnik *The Snow Party*

hatbands, or spots on horses. Often he creates interest in clothing, animals, and architecture with decorative pattern.

Zimnik's compositional arrangements are inspired. No matter how much or how little space remains after the type is accommodated, he can treat this space ingeniously. On some pages he competes with a sizable block of type and one's eye goes to the dynamic line first. There is a humorous quality in his line that suggests the spontaneity and rhythmic feeling of some of the Paul Klee drawings.

In *The Snow Party* (1959) Zimnik's drawings are clean, tiny, tidy, and elaborately detailed as to minutiae. Grains of wheat, tires on a truck, brick and shingle detail—everything is interpreted with awareness. His general outline statement is simple, while the special characteristics of the objects are most acutely perceived and translated. The page showing eighty-four grown-ups, seventeen children, seven babies, six dogs, a cat, a parakeet, a canary bird, and a little pet skunk, all within a "little old house," is one example. Besides the generalization of the whole, there are specific characterizations. The little old man and little old woman are wonderfully stolid country folk.

Zimnik alters his linear style to accommodate color in *The Bear on the Motorcycle* (1963). He is more the cartoonist here and less the designer. It seems he cannot design poorly nonetheless. His line is still tidy and precise but colored shapes predominate—larger shapes used with fewer groupings. The work is more gross, with more obvious substance and mass, and although efficient and full of style, it lacks the special inventive quality Zimnik shows in his feeling for line.

Summary

Emphasis, technique, and style vary among the foregoing illustrators and almost defy descriptive terminology. In much the same way that dance and music cannot be verbalized, a point is reached beyond which the visual arts cannot be discussed. They must be *seen*. Linear artists, color artists, and so on can be grouped, but the real differentiation must be made by the viewer as he confronts hundreds of varied illustrations.

The inherent value of the work of art is not a value implicit in the content, but a value assigned to the content by the compelling manner in which an artist has translated this object into an aesthetic visual reality. This transformation occurs by means of a visual language, an arrangement of symbols consisting of lines, colors, shapes, textures. But even when artists emphasize the same art elements, the manner in which this emphasis is made varies. For example, an interest in shapes is shared by Foreman, Balet, Schmid, Laurence, and Bemelmans. Yet each has treated this interest in a highly personal manner. Bemelmans' decorator-interest is not that of Schmid, who sculptures her shapes.

Zimnik and Sokol both use line, yet the tiny, precious, jewel-like precision of Zimnik's line in *The Snow Party* is not the same as Sokol's elegant, smooth, and fluid line in *Cats, Cats, Cats, Cats, Cats*. Nor is either one of them similar to Sidjakov's. The more artists we examine, the more variations we find. Sidjakov's line is graciously decorative. It is as controlled as Zimnik's, but for a different purpose. Sidjakov controls to decorate, to stripe, dot, or enhance in any way imaginable, while Zimnik controls for the purpose of accumulating mountains of detail to make a sweeping, gleeful statement. Mordvinoff's line is bold, expressive, and with an improvised quality that would be alien to Zimnik's work. Kepes' line in *Beasts from a Brush* is rhythmic and moving, in a sense similar to Sokol's, but identifiably different in treatment.

Artists' work with color also varies greatly. Yashima's treatment of color is in terms of light and dark and is combined with an abrupt foreshortening technique. Bemelmans uses color for background wash. Marcia Brown's color in

Cinderella adds to the softness of the textural quality. There is no one way or "right way" to use color; the way it is used by an artist depends upon the needs of the artist's interpretation.

We have said that François is a decorator, and that Sidjakov is a decorator also. Yet the difference between François's *Roland* and Sidjakov's *Baboushka* is evident. It is more than a difference in content. It is more than a difference in art element, for they both use line.

The value of the art work is not then a value inherent in the art elements any more than in the content, but rather a value assigned to these elements by the genius of the artist, by the way his own unique interpretation has been communicated. This uniqueness is a function of personality, and the limitations are those of the human personality. As the range of personality differences is limitless, so are the possibilities for using any of the art elements, either singly or in combination.

5

Book Design

THE OVERALL design of a picture book, the way all parts fit together, is the concern of the children's book editor, the designer or art director, the illustrator, and the author. Together they try to harmonize the illustrations with the text, and then the binding, typeface, endpapers, and so on with the illustrations. Every detail makes the book more attractive and unified.

Considering the illustrator in relation to book design, we can describe his fundamental problem in these terms: he tries to achieve a balance between the illustrative and decorative aspects of the pictures. If an equilibrium is reached between the representational and abstract elements of his art, the illustrations will clarify and extend the text simultaneously. It can be stated as an axiom that "the good illustration must be a good design irrespective of the text it accompanies," but at the same time, if the pictures have no real connection with the text, they cease being illustrations at all.[1] An illustrator must have images suggested to him by the reading of the text, and his illustrations must express the meaning of the text; however, if he effaces himself completely in trying to produce a literal representation, his work may lack character.[2] A relationship between text and illustration that is both relevant and unstereotyped is perhaps the first criterion for book design.

Other elements such as layout and typography will also contribute to or detract from the sense of harmony and wholeness. Hence they warrant the attention of a designer with specialized talent and training in these areas.

Origins of stories and illustrations have some influence upon the degree of correlation achieved, the unity of the book as a whole. When text and illustrations result from a collaboration of two individuals, it is usually the children's book editor who has selected a suitable illustrator and who deserves some credit for the successful partnership. Sometimes a writer and artist will collaborate many times, as in the case of the writer William Lipkind and the artist

Nicholas Mordvinoff. Then the task of the editor is simplified, although he may still have quite a lot to do with the overall design of the book (the choices the art director is making with respect to size, typeface, layout, and so on). In several instances, husband-and-wife teams have provided texts and illustrations, collaborating successfully on many books. Examples include Harve Zemach and his artist wife, Margot; Gene Zion and his artist wife, Margaret Bloy Graham; Louise Fatio and her artist husband, Roger Duvoisin.

Sometimes an artist will be his own storyteller, and on rare occasions a story will emerge from an entirely visual premise. For example, in *Inch by Inch* (1960) the story concerns an inchworm who measures things that need measuring, such as the long legs of a heron or the long tail of a pheasant. (He is only at a loss when it comes to measuring the nightingale's song.) The characters have a visual and a narrative role to play simultaneously. In the case of *A Firefly Named Torchy* (1970) by Bernard Waber, the visual and narrative demands are an inseparable unit also. Torchy's light is so bright that when he tries to glimmer he turns nighttime scenes into daytime scenes. Waber naturally uses the appropriate light and dark visual elements to make this point clear. In fact it's hard to imagine whether Waber made some drawings that suggested this story to him or whether the story came first.

This kind of close correlation is not very common. Usually the underlying premise of the story is nonvisual, and the illustrator's job is to work within the spirit of the text, while he is at the same time extending its emotional dimension, increasing its overall impact on the reader, and adding something which is delightful to the eye. Ideally, the artist engaged by a publisher to work on a given text will either grasp the author's intent and feel that he can express it honestly while at the same time expressing himself, or he will reject the assignment as not along his line of interest.

Good complementation of text cannot be prescribed by a neat formula. The harmony is felt primarily on a subjective and intuitive level. As Marcia Brown has stated: ". . . what is elusive [in the process of bookmaking] will remain so, since it is a subtle combination of personality, inner drive, and imagination in the author or illustrator himself."[3] Yet when a mood is captured by an illustrator with striking clarity, his method can be studied.

For example, Felix Hoffmann builds the mood of fairy tales in the romantic style. He is an exceptionally gifted craftsman, both in technique and control of line; and the expressive quality of his interpretations is well suited to the timeless feeling of the folk tale. In *Rapunzel* (1961) Hoffmann demonstrates his skill in building mood. In the magic forest scene, trees and animals are specifically defined, while still retaining the magic quality and fitting into the dreamlike and sentimental mood of the rest of the book. Hoffmann brings this forest close to the viewer by using the entire picture page for the tree trunks; this suggests great height, as they go out of the top of the page. He further accentuates the feeling of space by placing Rapunzel and the prince close to the viewer in the foreground, but still within the forest.

74

Hoffman *Rapunzel*

A sense of the dramatic is demonstrated in the illustration of a huge, exaggerated, dark form of the witch towering over the husband. Size dimensions are changed, yet the fearsome mood is retained in the picture of the witch carrying Rapunzel away. Here the witch is very small and is the only suggestion of movement in a cold, still, horizontal landscape.

Hoffmann achieves a sense of tragedy by strong contrasts of light and dark, as in a drawing of sad, shorn Rapunzel and the victorious witch. In this drawing the mood is heightened by framing the whole scene with a strong, wide, black line. The black outline merges into the dark dungeon walls on the upper right and left. The overall page design suggests that one is viewing the scene through a keyhole, adding to the feeling of secrecy and drama. Throughout *Rapunzel*, the illustrations complement the text and contribute to the unity of the book.

Unity is also produced through the craftsmanship of a book. Craftsmanship includes the artistic treatment of the binding, endpapers, paper quality and color, typeface, letter spacing, margins, blocking of type, type and illustration spacing. Such technical considerations can often enhance or diminish the meaning of the visual art. For example, a heavy black-and-white pattern of words in a text can make a thin, sensitive illustration seem inconsequential, as well as cause a dis-

continuity in the aesthetics of the page. In a similar fashion, a slight, delicate typeface can make the broad strokes of some illustrators' graphic art seem awkward and heavy.

Type arranged over the illustration usually does an injustice to the artwork and creates a haphazard effect on the page. It serves the practical purpose of keeping viewer and reader together (the child can follow the story with his eyes as he listens to his elders read it), but a line of type does not enhance the picture as a picture, unless it is conceived of as part of the overall design.

There are no rigid rules to follow in producing a consistent feeling in a book. What is needed is a creative appraisal of the bookmaking task at hand. Tomi Ungerer uses white type on black ground to balance effectively and boldly a strong opposing page in his book *Rufus* (1961). In Evaline Ness's *All in the Morning Early* (1963) an italic typeface is used for the rhyming refrain, and roman Bembo type for the story line. This variation is well suited to the mood of the book, and there is no interference visually, for the italicized and regular typefaces complement the quality of the line in the illustrations. All the pages are framed with a color edge of blue, brown, or gray, tastefully completing the page design. Nonny Hogrogian, in *Sir Ribbeck of Ribbeck of Havelland* (1969), allows a comfortable amount of space for her woodcuts and combines them with the endpapers, title page, and typeface which together make a well-composed book.

William Wondriska is a designer-illustrator, and his book *Which Way to the Zoo?* (1962) gives the impression of an artist's sketchbook. His drawings have the spontaneity of on-the-spot sketches in thin and thick black lines on brown wrapping-type paper.

In *The Tomato Patch* (1964), a story about two warring medieval kingdoms, Wondriska is interested in the pattern and decoration of medieval castles. The front endpapers show flat decorative spears and arrows which are treated as patterns of alternating black on gray and white on gray. The back endpapers boldly repeat a red, contourless tomato shape. The two designs are interesting in their contrast. Both are strongly stated, but the spear and arrow design is more rhythmic in overall quality while the tomato design is boldly staccato.

John Burningham designs marvelous endpapers of textured pink ground on which he places a pattern of dark brown leaves interlaced with lighter red-brown fox shapes. This style, in *Harquin: The Fox Who Went Down to the Valley* (1968), is not continued anywhere else in the book, and although there is no rule which says that it must be, it makes for a visual discontinuity to announce a style and then do nothing with it. This kind of discontinuity is also noticeable in Uri Shulevitz's *The Fool of the World and the Flying Ship* (1968).

One of the most common design problems is seen in Leo Lionni's *Tico and the Golden Wings* (1964). This intriguingly illustrated book is a poorly constructed one, cheaply bound and printed in such a way as to allow insufficient margins. As a result, Lionni's art does not have an adequate showcase.

Continuity problems, arising from the different emphasis in two facing pages, are also all too frequent. In *Celestino Piatti's Animal ABC* (1966), Piatti apparently created the animals individually with little or no thought for their arrangement on the double pages. This results in disparate statements facing each other and creating an unnecessary clash. For example, the bear and the chameleon are such dissimilar shapes and colors that they make a poor double page. Also, the quetzal and rhinoceros drawings interfere with each other in an inexcusable manner. The quetzal page is decorative, colorful, and fanciful—the most complex page in the book. It needs the relief of white ground around it, not the large mass of a brown-black-gray rhino which throws the other side of the book out of scale. The lion and the nightingale survive this kind of problem because of the substantial amount of white ground between them. This isolates them into two distinct visual areas.

The center fold in a double-page spread also presents difficulties to the designer-illustrator, especially when a tight, heavy-duty stitching is used. For example, the fold nearly ruins a beautiful page depicting a lion's head in Yutaka Sugita's *Have You Seen My Mother?* (1969), but in the same book the strength of the value contrast in a zebra's stripes overcomes the shadow of another page fold and the distortion it creates.

The quality of the total design varies widely in picture books, and examples of good design are not as plentiful as one would expect. Publishing costs account for this to some degree; however, children's book editor Jean Poindexter Colby minimizes the cost problem:

> Money is a factor but not as much of a one as it is supposed to be. . . . No, book designing demands "only" interest, imagination, artistic ability and mental integrity to be good. It is first and foremost a creative task and beautiful can be the results.[4]

6

Literary Elements

THE SOUND of words, the lively progression of a story, and its dramatic contents are as intriguing to the picture-book audience as the works of graphic artists. Young children respond wholeheartedly to the lilt of verse, the excitement of conflict, the quirks of human personality, and the many humorous incongruities and fanciful plot inventions in picture books.

It need hardly be added that excellent writers are seldom graphic artists as well. Many writers have been their own illustrators, but not the sort that are important in the long-term history of book art. This fact requires some explanation and a word about the cartoonist as storyteller.

Engaging characters and imaginative narratives seem to flow from the pen of good cartoonists as readily as the simple drawings which make these narratives visible. Perhaps the cartoon drawings and the stories are imagined simultaneously, or at least in close conjunction with each other. In any case, good stories for children have often had this kind of origin, and although the illustrations do not offer great aesthetic richness in themselves, we can find in the stories the ideal qualities for pleasing young audiences.

The cartoon illustrations have quite a different function from illustrations discussed so far in this study; they have a narrative function more than a truly visual one. The pictures are used by the child as he would use a toy, as a substitution for something with which his imagination is engaged, but he is not being stimulated, stirred, astonished, and delighted in a purely visual way. This is what picture-book art that is pure art can do. It gives the viewer an experience in seeing that is unique. The child crosses "the frontier into that new region which the pictorial art as such has added to the world."[1]

But children can be engaged by the literary qualities in a book and at the same time become caught up in the narrative qualities of the pictures. This means they are using them as substitutes for what is being referred to in the story. Children return to good texts (usually stories) again and again and to the accompanying narrative-type illustrations; but without the imaginative and skillful use of the art elements discussed in Chapter 3, there will be no compulsion to return to the illustrations for their own sake as visual treats. If a picture has nothing but narrative usefulness, it dies after the first viewing, except as a reminder of the pleasant actions and characters of a story.

The characters and actions, however, have their own importance, and along with other literary elements need to be evaluated by critics as specifically as the graphic elements.

One's first impression of a picture-book text is that it is one of the shortest of all narrative forms. In fact, written texts often consist of little more than a series of captions connected with a series of illustrations. Still, these brief statements are intended to be read aloud and to carry, in many instances, a considerable weight of characterization and emotion.

Students of children's literature often approach these brief statements with a concern about the words used, the difficulty of the vocabulary. They seem convinced that every child must be familiar with the exact meaning of every word he hears. They are as worried about this today as they were in 1937 when Frances Clarke Sayers made this comment in a speech before the American Library Association:

> The emphasis on word content of a book has a pernicious influence upon students, teachers, and librarians. There is difficulty in getting them to read the book, to discover what the author has to say. They are concerned with what words he has used. . . . I have seen teachers and librarians look at books as though they were pieces of merchandise, scanning the page for words—not ideas—and condemning them upon that basis.[2]

Easy comprehension is, admittedly, one facet of a text, but the style of the writer, his originality, dramatic sense, feeling for characterization, and his sense of humor are of even greater importance. If a word obscures the development of the story, this is clearly a problem for the storyteller, for he will have to interrupt the tale to make some explanation. But good writers do not use words which will obstruct the comprehension of a crucial plot point. Rather, the richness of their language helps create rhythms, moods, settings, and highly differentiated characters. All these qualities are within the appreciation of a young child, although he cannot explain them analytically. He is not limited to one response—the mere understanding of plot. He chants strange words, mimics his favorite characters, and clearly reacts to the overall mood pervading a story.

Originality of Concept

Originality, the sheer quantity of it, is one of the most astonishing features of children's literature. We find millions of cats marching behind a very old man, each expecting to become his pet (*Millions of Cats* by Wanda Gág, 1928); a big-hearted moose allowing his horns to become the lodging place of a turtle, fox, bear, and numerous other creatures (*Thidwick, the Big-hearted Moose* by Dr. Seuss, 1948); mice turning the wire from sprung mousetraps into pieces of sculpture (*Norman the Doorman* by Don Freeman, 1959); a bird unraveling a dog's rose-decorated sweater and weaving the yarn into a rose-decorated nest (*No Roses for Harry* by Gene Zion, 1958)—scores of ingenious ideas, characters, and episodes.

Some of this invention occurs in the area of conception rather than treatment. The whole plot concept can be so unusual that the reader or listener is utterly amazed by the underlying idea and finds it a kind of revelation. This kind of originality, the kind that is integral to the entire conception of the story, is the most creative and the most rare.

Fantasies are more richly endowed with this kind of originality than other genres. *The Red Carpet* (1948) by Rex Parkin tells of a hotel carpet that runs through the town of its own accord and over hill and dale to meet a visiting dignitary when his boat docks.

> And there on the ferryboat *Annabel Lou*
> Was the Duke of Sultana and his retinue!
> "My goodness!" he beamed, when he saw the display.
> "This is a tremendous surprise, I must say!. . . .
> A whole squad of police, and a red carpet too,
> To welcome me here, from the Hotel Bellevue!"

In *The 500 Hats of Bartholomew Cubbins* (1938) by Dr. Seuss we see what can happen when a hat becomes bewitched and will not allow itself to be removed even when the command is given: "Hats off to the King!"

Imagination is a fundamental quality in any well-conceived story, but it has a broader definition than is suggested by fanciful invention or novel detail. Imagination can refer to whatever presents "the real more fully and truly than it appears to the senses and in its ideal or universal character." (*Webster's New Collegiate Dictionary*). Thus a story such as *Blueberries for Sal* (1948) by Robert McCloskey can be appreciated for its quality of imagination, its insights into the experience of a very young child. In McCloskey's story, a child and a bear cub, both on family berry-picking expeditions, become so preoccupied with eating blueberries that they inadvertently get mixed up, and each one tags along behind the wrong mother. The absent-mindedness of small children, their greediness over a taste they like, their confidence in Mother even when she is represented by another member of the animal family—these universal characteristics of the three-year-old were noticed by a writer of more than average perception and appreciation of children. Mixing up the two protagonists was a simple plot device, but it provided the author with a framework for depicting the character of a small child. At the same time it produced a miniature adventure for the listeners.

Whether the young reader's early contacts are with stories of a fanciful nature, or those offering an imaginative view of reality, books supply him with that extension of his being which good fiction provides. On the other hand, the child with little exposure to storytelling lacks the shared experience that gives his imagination wider range. As C. S. Lewis remarked about the unliterary man, "he may be full of goodness and good sense but he inhabits a tiny world."[3]

Drama

Drama is based upon conflict within or between characters or between a character and his environment. It tends to stir emotions and hold the reader in a state of involvement until the point of the story has been made. Feelings of sympathy, tension, and excitement arise from the dramatic incidents in literature, and having an occasion to exercise these emotions is one of the dividends we derive from good reading. Elizabeth Bowen has written:

> One of the insufficiencies of routine existence is the triviality of the demands it makes on us. Largely unused remain our funds of pity, spontaneous love, unenvious admiration or selfless anger.[4]

It does not take as much drama to stir the feelings of a child as it does to affect an adult. In fact, picture books must be read in the company of young children in order for adults to appreciate how little tension is needed. The most minute intimation of conflict is usually sufficient.

In the story *Jeanne-Marie Counts Her Sheep* (1951) by Françoise (a mere counting book at first glance), the heroine, Jeanne-Marie, envisions all the things she could buy if her sheep, Patapon, would give birth to one lamb or two, and so on, up to seven. There is a plaintive tone throughout, stemming from the story's one dramatic circumstance: limitation. As it turns out there is only one lamb born, and it makes just enough wool for a new pair of socks for Jeanne-Marie, not enough to trade for shoes or a red hat or a donkey or "a little house with a blue room for me and a carpet for you, Patapon."

Unequal supply and demand are only touched upon in *Jeanne-Marie Counts Her Sheep*, but the conflict is sufficient to produce a genuine feeling of sympathy for the heroine. The child also senses that the problem of unfulfilled wishes is a common one.

In *Make Way for Ducklings* (1941) by Robert McCloskey, it is the condition of homelessness and a hazardous journey that captures attention and causes grave concern for two mallard ducks and their eight ducklings. Loneliness is the plight of the Happy Lion in Louise Fatio's book and Mister Muster in *A Zoo for Mister Muster* (1962) by Arnold Lobel. Hunger, jealousy, various forms of persecution—in fact the most basic human problems—are handled at a child's level and carry a strong dramatic impact.

But it is the treatment as much as the narrative line which must be examined by the critic. Dramatic quality is enhanced by the shaping of a plot, and the skillful writer will therefore tighten and balance the structure of his story. As in the

82

folk tale, the plot issue can be announced early, and the pacing can be swift. The climax can be strong as well as plausible.

Since young children are usually unsophisticated, they can accept melodrama as readily as drama. And in fact, in a brief picture-book story, the treatment of character and situation is bound to be somewhat melodramatic, that is, grossly oversimplified. A quick, picturesque encounter between good and evil is a familiar pattern. The listener feels a thrill of excitement as the danger or dilemma is introduced, a sense of moral indignation when he meets the villain, and a feeling of happiness when, at the conclusion, all the right punishments and rewards are apportioned to the characters.

Yet some picture books have a more melodramatic quality than others, and the several Mellops stories by Tomi Ungerer are useful examples. The Mellops pig family, in *The Mellops' Go Spelunking* (1963), find a crevice in the ground and decide to go spelunking to discover what is at the bottom. They experience several disasters in the cavern below, culminating in an encounter with smugglers. These villains appear rather arbitrarily and for the obvious purpose of generating more excitement. On the other hand, in *The Tale of Peter Rabbit* (1902) by Beatrix Potter the danger is integral to the entire story concept. We would have no tale at all without Peter's character as an adventurer and the inevitable antagonism of Mr. McGregor, the gardener. In this story the climax builds by a logical progression, not through mere contrivance.

A redeeming aspect of melodrama in picture books is its union with whimsy. Author-artist Tomi Ungerer appears to be teasing his readers in the Mellops stories, depicting danger that is really only mock danger. His illustrations as well as his texts emphasize the humor. One of the four pig brothers is always seen chewing on a flower, even as he helps load the captured villains into barrels and rolls them off to the police station. The brothers have the light-hearted names of Isidor, Casimir, Ferdinand, and Felix. Mother pig is a traditional domestic figure, whipping up her special whipped-cream pie upon each return of the heroes. The game of mock danger and mock fear is half the fun in these books, and children go along with it in the spirit of play.

Overcautious adults sometimes fear a detrimental effect from moments of tension in children's books. They cannot distinguish the difference between drama as it appears in literature and the sensationalism of a detective-style comic book. The thing to remember is that a good writer tempers conflict as he shapes it into narrative form, as he weaves it inextricably and in proper balance with other qualities. The child hears a picture-book story in one sitting and in all probability conceives of it as a whole. It would be a mistake to fasten attention on just one literary element and not notice the interplay of qualities which together are creating the child's response.

P. M. Pickard, a British psychiatrist, discusses the use children make of violence in literature from a psychological standpoint. She advocates the oral telling of folk tales to children, tales which usually have much more drama than the average picture book. She argues that children have to repress many desires in their early adjustments to people and circumstances, that young children are bound to make frequent mistakes as to what is acceptable and what is not. Pickard notes that repressed wishes are very energetic and require great exertion in being held down, energy that the child needs for other purposes. Emotions of fear, wonder, love, and hate in stories give children another opportunity to deal with these feelings. They are seen with detachment, and since the child feels no personal responsibility, there is no serious anxiety in this new encounter. He looks again at the situation, now in changed form, and considers whether or not the emotion must indeed be rejected in its entirety.[5] A dramatic story can therefore be a strengthening experience for a child, and a right sense of proportion in the whole work a psychological advantage.

It should also be noted that in the vast majority of picture books, humor enters into some aspect of the story, and the most timid listener is affected by it, even while dramatic situations are building up in the plot.

Plot

To analyze and judge the plot of a picture book one has to be willing to appreciate its simplicity. Other features such as progression, climax, and resolution are important, but simplicity and brevity are characteristic of books for a young audience, and compactness is an advantage.

Complexity need not be a higher value than simplicity in the art of narrative. As seen in the folk tale, when a simple plot has been perfected in terms of structure, the story's form becomes so perfectly balanced and well defined that it is an end in itself; its movements and juxtapositions are pleasing in almost the same way the composition of a painting is pleasing. At the same time, the compactness adds a sense of vitality and dramatic intensity.

In the picture book, each incident is often parallel with the others in presentation, and this repetition is extended even to the words that are used. Especially in books for the youngest audience, the manner of unraveling the plot may be through patterns and refrains. There are no distractions in the form of subplots or extraneous characters. And as in the case of the folk tale, the method used by the storyteller is dramatic rather than descriptive. The child has the sense of being in the presence of the action, of having a direct view as each scene is acted out.

An example of ultra-simplicity of plot and the extensive use of rhythmic patterns and refrains is the story *Millions of Cats* (1928) by Wanda Gág. It resembles the brief folk anecdote in which the body of the tale is filled out with repetitive verses and parallel incidents. The construction is so compact that within half a dozen sentences we learn everything we will ever know about the characters, their location, their problem, and their plan to solve it. A "very old woman" says she wishes she had a cat and her husband, a "very old man," says he'll find her one. The rest is all rhythm and pattern centering around the selection of the pet. As the cats follow the man home they stop twice: each has one drop of water (leaving the pond dry) and one blade of grass (leaving the hillside bare). The refrain provides a unifying, chant-like effect:

> Cats here, cats there,
> Cats and kittens everywhere,
> Hundreds of cats,
> Thousands of cats,
> Millions and billions and trillions of cats.

A ferocious battle among the cats culminates in the impossible, nonsensical, and wondrous fact that they "eat each other up," that is, all except one kitten. This is a proper climax because it's strong enough to enable the listener to feel deeply about the resolution. The child has a sense of relief and satisfaction because the one modest kitten has found a good home. There can be no literal awareness of cats "eating each other up" because such a happening is clearly impossible; it's as fantastic as the rest of the story.

A longer and more complicated plot is found in Virginia Kahl's *The Duchess Bakes A Cake* (1955), but a basic clarity and simplicity are still characteristic. The issue to be resolved stems in the first place from the scatterbrained character of the Duchess. She's so optimistic and gay and light-headed (in fact, in the whole family their "brains were such/ That they couldn't think often,/ And hadn't thought much") that she puts everything imaginable into her batter and tops it off with "an improper proportion of leaven." The cake rises all the way up to the clouds despite her desperate efforts to hold it down by sitting on it.

> Her cries brought the family, one and other,
> "Come girls," said the Duke,
> "Say good-bye to your mother."

The problem is, of course, how to get the Duchess down. Attempts are made to shoot her down with a catapult, among other things, until at last Gunhilde, the youngest of the thirteen daughters, gets hungry and cries for her dinner.

> Of course! That would do it, and it could be a treat;
> They could bring down the Duchess if they started to eat.
> "How lovely!" the Duchess said. "Come, let us sup.
> "I'll start eating down; you start eating up."

This method works, but the entire ducal family and the King and Queen who are guests end up noticeably overweight. The whole thing has a superb logic, and the author lets just the right amount of suspense build up in the plot before she unravels it.

The refrain,

> "All I wanted to make
> Was a lovely light luscious delectable cake,"

punctuates the story intermittently, but it is never used without a logical context. The ingenious, fantastic, plot line holds the reins of the listeners' attention, while the rhyming lines and the refrain add to the mood, the unity, and the musical dimension.

Style

Style is the most difficult and intriguing quality in literature. Definitions run all the way from Buffon's "style is the man himself," to F. L. Lucas' description of style as that which "endows language . . . with persuasiveness and power."[6] Young children seem to feel the persuasiveness and power of language primarily through such qualities as rhythm (often in the form of repetition), concreteness, and the impression of hearing an actual voice.

Repetitious patterns of sound helped make the folk tale easily remembered and transmitted by word of mouth, but they also must have pleased the audiences of the ancient storytellers just as they please children today. In fact, there are examples of primitive literary repetition which some of the most sophisticated audiences would find hard to resist. (John Greenway cites examples in his book *Literature Among the Primitives*.[7])

The amount of repetition in a picture book text varies widely, having at one extreme books for the very young such as *Pop Corn and Ma Goodness* (1969) by Edna Mitchell Preston. This text has the character of a folk rhyme with onomatopoeic word play and many repeated and accumulated phrases. The story concerns a frontier family:

> Now Pop he chops firewood a-chippitty choppetty
> And Ma redds the house up a-mippitty moppetty
> The kids—oh they're brats all a-snippitty snoppetty
> They whup one another a-bippitty boppetty
> Old hounddog—they chase him a-yippitty yoppetty
> > All doon the hill.

In the story *Away Went Wolfgang* (1954) by Virginia Kahl we find simply the use of parallel descriptions, as when the dog's mistress says, "All right Wolfgang. Off we go!"

> And Wolfgang was off like a shot—upsetting the cat, scaring the geese, spilling the milk, and the old lady hanging on for dear life.

Since Wolfgang is an extremely rambunctious milk-cart dog, this happens quite a few times.

The more concrete the language of the storyteller, the more pleasure for the listener, for concrete words create vivid images and sometimes unusual sounds. Too often the picture-book writer makes the mistake of using general terms in the attempt to find easy ones. Nothing will remove the life and vitality from a text so quickly.

86

Rumer Godden, who writes for both children and adults, rightly insists that the expressive beauty of words is not wasted on the young; rather, children glory in "new words, long words, euphonious phrases." Words, she says, have "shades and shades of meanings," and some are more effective than others in communicating the essence of the things they describe, even to sounding like them. She summarizes here a basic principle:

> Children's books are made with fewer words than books for adults, so that this already imposes a discipline on the writer, as each word becomes more important. Added to this, such books are usually meant to be read aloud, so the rhythm is doubly integral. No panel of philologists, however learned, can know what words the writer will need. He needs not the narrowest, but the widest range of English from which to choose.[8]

Miss Godden's encounters with children verify this point of view. Speaking of a three-year-old, she said:

> I remember one who could not sleep, stamping up and down the corridor repeating a phrase from *The Tailor of Gloucester* by Beatrix Potter: "No more twist . . . no more twist," which soothed him as a lullaby would have done.

On another occasion she was walking in a poor London district and encountered some seven- or eight-year-olds:

> . . . in the drab street, that chill November day, they were chanting a refrain from W. J. Turner's poem "Romance": "Shining Popocatepetl! Shining Popocatepetl!"[9]

Anyone working with children can collect similar examples. A two-year-old recently amazed his mother by retaining over a long interval the words "sack of stars" from *Bruno Munari's ABC* (1960). Before she could read the words, he was eagerly chanting this phrase:

> a Sack
> of Stars
> and Snow
> for
> Santa Claus.

It apparently flooded his mind at the sight of a particular illustration.

One of the delights of *The Duchess Bakes a Cake* is its sprinkling of concrete, euphonious words: "pummel," "catapult," "billowed," "minstrel," "embroidery." In *Mr. Gumpy's Outing* (1971) by John Burningham, barnyard and child characters "squabble," "tease," "trample," "bleat," and "muck about."

Writers for young children sometimes make the mistake of oversimplifying their sentence construction also. Sentences that are very short tend to be uniform as well and monotonous to listen to. The redeeming element is the use of dialogue, which adds a distinct, specific impression of different personalities.

Crisp, naturalistic dialogue adds enormously to the quality of a picture book. The impression of actually hearing a voice is carried to the reader; a sense of personality reaches him rather than just words from a remote narrator. And producing this oral sensation is one of the highest skills in the art of narration. At one time, critics like Molbech in Denmark viewed this quality as a defect rather than a virtue. "It's not writing, it's talking," complained Molbech about the writings of Hans Christian Andersen.[10] Passages like the following (from *The Steadfast Tin Soldier* [1953]) were not always viewed as giving the Danish language "grace and color, the freshness of simplicity."

> "Where can I be going to now?" thought he. "Aye, this is the troll's doing. Ah, dear, if that little lady was here in the boat, it might be twice as dark for all I cared!" Just then came up a big water-rat who lived under the culvert.
> "Got a pass? Out with your pass!"
> But the Tin Soldier said nothing, and held his rifle tighter than ever. The boat rushed on, and the rat after it.
> Ugh! How it gnashed its teeth and called out to the chips and straws: "Stop him! Stop him! he hasn't paid the toll! he hasn't shown his pass!"

Another critic, Georg Brandes, appreciated Andersen's style and felt it was a particularly suitable one for children's stories. Brandes said:

> Whoever . . . addresses himself in writing to a child must have at his command the changeful cadence, the sudden pauses, the descriptive gesticulations, the awe-inspiring mien, the smile which betrays the happy turn of affairs, the jest, the caress, and the appeal to rouse the flagging attention— all these he must endeavor to weave into his diction, and as he cannot directly sing, paint, or dance the occurrences to the child, he must imprison within his prose the song, the picture, and the pantomimic movements, that they may lie there like forces in bonds, and rise up in their might as soon as the book is opened.[11]

Anita Hewett tells a tale in *The Little White Hen* (1963), capturing in her prose the sound of a storyteller's voice:

> Once upon a time a little white hen was scratching in the farmyard, when she found a piece of paper, covered all over with squiggly marks.
> "Tuck-a-luck-luck," said the little white hen. "It must be a letter. I wonder what it says."
> The little white hen put on her spectacles. But she could not read the letter.
> "I shall take it to the king. *He* knows everything."

There are few metaphors in picture-book literature because the story moves too rapidly and attention focuses on events rather than description. Also the profusion of illustrations makes verbal description unnecessary. There are exceptions in mood pieces or the kinds of narratives in which the writer is trying to convey the actuality of objects rather than the speed of events. But similes and other descriptive devices are usually confined to closing or opening paragraphs as in the beginning of *Mazel and Shlimazel; or The Milk of a Lioness* (1967) by Isaac Bashevis Singer:

> In a faraway land, on a sunny spring day, the sky was as blue as the sea, and the sea was as blue as the sky, and the earth was green and in love with them both.

In a mood piece such as *The Moon Jumpers* (1959) by Janice Udry, the writer may depend upon the use of metaphor and fragments of potential verse: "And the balloon of a moon grows and grows," "The sun is tired. It goes down the sky into the drowsy hills," "The wind chimes stir."

Writers of prose achieve their rhythmical effects from anticipation, according to I. A. Richards, and "as a rule this anticipation is unconscious." He explains that "sequences of syllables both as sounds and as images of speech-movements leave the mind ready for certain further sequences rather than for others. . . . Prose . . . is accompanied by a very much vaguer and more indeterminate expectancy than verse."[12] But sharpness of imagery, variety, and the rhythm that produces ease in reading a passage—these qualities can never be neglected by writers of even the simplest works of prose.

The writer who tells his story in verse has additional concerns, namely the pitfalls of forced rhyme and uneven rhythm. Since the young child's expectation is to hear a tale, the form of the story should reinforce that expectation, not create an interference. Writers who have decided to use the artifice of rhyme should be able to produce that kind of lilt that stamps a verse indelibly on memory, but at the same time holds the listener's attention to the narrative. Accented beats falling at regular intervals have this effect.

If this kind of rhythm seems monotonous to an adult and somewhat tedious to perform, he can place his emphasis upon the dramatic content of the story. This helps him keep his own interest alive. But even then, adults seldom read well unless they allow the child's peculiar pleasure in verse to touch them. In presenting picture books, sophisticated adults must be flexible and sensitive enough to catch for a moment the child's joyous response to repetitive sounds, as well as slapstick humor, melodrama, and fantasy.

In a rhyming text words need to be chosen which are as logical for the content of the narrative as they would be in a work of prose; they should seem almost inevitable. Otherwise the listener is distracted and annoyed as he tries to catch the story line through a maze of unnatural words. The only workable forced rhymes are those which are comical, and to produce these takes a rare talent.

Ogden Nash was famous for this knack in the field of adult verse, and children have Dr. Seuss, as, for example, in *The Sneetches and Other Stories* (1961):

> Now, the Star-Belly Sneetches
> Had bellies with stars.
> The Plain-Belly Sneetches
> Had none upon thars. . . .
>
> Then up came McBean with a very sly wink
> And he said, "Things are not quite as bad as you think.
> So you don't know who's who. That is perfectly true.
> But come with me, friends. Do you know what I'll do?
> I'll make you, again, the best Sneetches on beaches
> And all it will cost you is ten dollars eaches."

These playful changes in spelling, tenses, and sounds engage a child's sense of humor, a rowdy sense which is not offended by "bellies with stars."

Another good example of picture-book verse is Phyllis McGinley's *Lucy McLockett* (1959), the story of a six-year-old who loses things:

> One autumn morning
> On the way to school,
> With the trees bright red and the sky, bright blue,
> Can you imagine?
> She lost her shoe!
> She was scuffling, ruffling,
> Through the sweet
> Hills of leaves along the street,
> When off it came, like a fish unhooked.
> Well! She never found it
> Though she looked and *looked*.
> The First Grade
> Couldn't help but grin
> When Lucy McLockett
> Came limping in,
> Late and grimy, her hair ribbon gone,
> One shoe off,
> One shoe on.

Besides her clothes, she loses her temper and finally in a large department store:

> . . . before you could say,
> "Jack-Something-or-Other!"
> Lucy McLockett
> Had lost her *mother!*

Humor

Humor is usually an aspect of either style or concept, but it takes a variety of forms. In "The Sneetches" by Dr. Seuss we saw how humorous word play was part of the author's rhyme scheme. In *The Story About Ping* (1933) by Marjorie Flack, children are amused when the author provides this elaborate description of the hero's family:

> Once upon a time there was a beautiful young duck named Ping. Ping lived with his mother and his father and two sisters and three brothers and eleven aunts and seven uncles and forty-two cousins.

Polly Cameron exploits the sounds of rhymes for a humorous effect in her book *I Can't, Said the Ant* (1961). Various utensils and groceries comment upon the plight of a broken teapot and the attempts of an ant to help her.

> "What's all the clatter?" asked the platter.
> "Teapot fell," said the dinner bell.
> "Teapot broke," said the artichoke.
> "She went kerplop!" said the mop.
> "Is she dead?" asked the bread.
> "Just a break," said the steak. . . .
> "Push her up," said the cup.
> "I can't," said the ant.

Such remarks continue for many pages, interspersed with scenes about fixing the teapot, and besides the humor of the rhymes, the sheer number of items in the kitchen and their different comments take on nonsensical proportions.

> "Don't break her," said the shaker.
> "Don't choke her," said the poker.
> "She'll crash!" said the trash.
> "I can't look," said the book.
> "I can't bear it," said the carrot.

Inspired incongruities are sometimes the underlying basis for a plot, as in *Anatole and the Cat* (1957) by Eve Titus. Here the cheese expert (a mouse named Anatole) gets so upset by the presence of a cat in the cheese factory that he gives bad advice to the factory workers. Instead of attaching his usual notes to the cheeses ("not creamy enough" or "another pinch of salt") he suggests wildly incongruous combinations: "add some pickled strawberries," "use crushed jelly-beans," "wrap it in a banana peel." Since Anatole is a mouse, it is logical for him to suffer such a total loss of wits when threatened by a cat. The nonsense here is entirely integral with the plot, not tacked on.

Slapstick is perhaps the most elementary form of humor, showing some sort of physical chaos or the exaggerated discomfiture of a character. But the chaos must be related to something specific, to other points in the story. *The Good Man and His Good Wife* (1962) by Ruth Krauss is a story about a husband who cures his wife of the habit of moving the furniture around. His method is to get tired of "the same things in the same place" himself:

> He put his shoe on his head.
> He wore his garters around his neck.
> He tied his necktie around his knee. . . .
> He sat on the breakfast table, ate his napkin,
> and wiped his face on a biscuit.

Characterization

Character portrayals in picture books are also of various kinds. Animal characters are often really human in everything except appearance, retaining just a suggestion of animal nature. There are also animal characters who remain close to animal nature, and of course there are purely human characters.

It doesn't matter which of these types the author chooses, so long as he is consistent in his treatment and so long as the characterization is credible. To a young child it is not at all incredible for a character to act just like a person and yet be a rabbit. This suspension of disbelief is second nature to the young and causes no confusion at all. However, when strictly adult ideas or emotions are expressed by child characters, or animals representing child characters, the characterization is not credible in the eyes of any reader, young or old.

It is extraordinary that an author, using a highly compressed form in which to tell his story, has room to suggest character at all or to create personalities with any distinctiveness. And in fact characterization in picture books is usually a case of one idiosyncrasy being exaggerated and used as the basis for a whole chain of actions. The exaggeration makes the story humorous and light-hearted in tone, while at the same time the inevitability of behavior makes the character engaging and memorable.

An author like Beatrix Potter manages to reveal personality in numerous subtle ways and usually through action and dialogue. This does not mean that there is an elaborate or introspective treatment of character in her books. However, the subtle differentiations heighten the interest of her stories and provide a model for picture-book authors. In some Potter books we find that a goose is scatterbrained, a fox sly, a mouse busy—characteristics that literature has long attached to these animals. But Miss Potter's special talent is in depicting a wide range of human characteristics through animal characters. This she does with whimsy as well as sympathy, and with an amazing economy of language.

Mrs. Tittlemouse, in *The Tale of Mrs. Tittlemouse* (1910), is a mousewife like many of her human counterparts, for she is obsessed with housekeeping.

> Mrs. Tittlemouse was a most terribly tidy particular little mouse, always sweeping and dusting the soft sandy floors.

Sometimes a beetle lost its way in the passages.

"Shuh! shuh! little dirty feet!" said Mrs. Tittlemouse, clattering her dust-pan.

When Mr. Jackson, a bullfrog, paid a visit with his wet feet and dripping coattails, Mrs. Tittlemouse treated him with cool hospitality and "went around with a mop." It was natural that Mr. Jackson should be wet since he lived in a drain in a dirty wet ditch, but other characteristics are attributed to him as well. Miss Potter has made him the epitome of all dull-witted, ill-mannered gentlemen callers. He sits "all over a small rocking chair," goes rummaging in all the cupboards as well as the pantry and larder looking for tidbits that suit him, and is even too thick-skulled and insensitive to be offended when Mrs. Tittlemouse later excludes him from a party and makes the doorway smaller to keep him out.

As Dorothy White has written, "If a child read nothing else he would have experienced in them [the Beatrix Potter books] the basic human types and the basic human emotions."[13]

In *The Story of Ferdinand* (1936) by Munro Leaf, character and plot are so inextricably bound together that the child gets the advantages of both without having to listen to lengthy descriptions. As a youngster, Ferdinand the bull was a nonconformist who preferred sitting quietly and smelling flowers to running around and butting the other bulls. This worried Ferdinand's mother for a while, but she finally came to realize that he was not lonesome and "because she was an understanding mother, even though she was a cow, she let him just sit there and be happy." The hero's character doesn't change even when he is a full-grown bull, but when he accidentally sits on a bumblebee in the presence of a Madrid bull-picking committee, the story is provided with its plot. A case of mistaken identity is the central issue, for the peaceful Ferdinand, when he comes to Madrid, is scarcely the wild creature that the committee thought they observed in the field.

Harry, in *Harry, the Dirty Dog* (1956) by Gene Zion, is a carefree individualist who goes off on a fling in the mud when the mood strikes him, but like a young child, he needs home and security as the day ends. Another facet of Harry's personality is his strong personal taste in clothing. In *No Roses for Harry* (1958) this independent-minded dog receives a sweater with an effeminate rose design, and his problem is how to get rid of it diplomatically. He must not offend the grandmother who knitted it.

Many of the texts mentioned so far could be separated from their illustrations and depicted by other artists without any great loss to the spirit of the books. But this is difficult to imagine in the Harry books, which are illustrated by the author's wife, Margaret Bloy Graham. Harry seems no more separable from the embodiment given him by Margaret Bloy Graham than Snoopy would be from the line drawings Charles Schulz creates in the comic strip *Peanuts*. Harry is a mongrel whose character is immensely enhanced by his cartoonist-illustrator.

Whatever the device for expressing personality or distinctive character, the task of the picture-book writer is to know his characters so well that even without direct statements about their nature, some suggestion of individuality will shine through. In many instances it will be only implied in the text through action and dialogue, while it is expressed more fully with pen or brush by the illustrator. But if the reader leaves the story with nothing to remember but the plot, he has missed one of the real pleasures of fiction: character portrayal. The more distinctive and true to human nature, the more memorable the character will be and the longer his life span in children's literature.

7

Outstanding Narrative Writers

Wᴿɪᴛᴇʀs during the last half century have been creating original narrative picture books to the point where we can now refer to a body of literature in this category. Some examples have been described in the previous chapter, but there are many others which should be mentioned for their strong appeal to children: for their ability to delight young audiences with a combination of imaginative invention, characterization, drama, and humor. Some are already commonly referred to as "classics," and, along with the folk tales, deserve a permanent place in children's libraries.

The writers of these small classics are not basically different from other good writers; like all artists they must have something to say and feel keenly about saying it. And the children's author is not as limited as one might at first think by the limited range of the young child's experience. If an author has something to say that is playful, fanciful, nonsensical, incongruous, ingenious, or charged with sympathy, a very young audience is an ideal one. Most children are highly responsive and sensitive to expressions of this sort.

The more demanding qualification in the picture-book author is that innate rhythmic sense which brings distinction and vitality to a short literary work. Writers vary widely in their possession of this gift, but without having it in some measure, an author's stories will seem quite dead beside the hundreds of folk tales whose rhythms and forms have been polished over centuries. A picture-book text has little reason to exist unless it can successfully compete with the imaginative and structural beauty of the many anonymous tales which, in length and content, suit the same young audience.

Folk tales are unsurpassed on any scale which seeks to measure pure imaginative force and beauty of form. In these areas folk narratives serve as excellent models for the contemporary children's writer. However, there are several reasons why some traditional tales can be adapted to the picture-book format better than others. The examples from folk literature in this chapter indicate some of the best uses that can be made of the illustrated folk tale.

Whether stories are contemporary or have their origins buried in the distant past, the fact that lively events are narrated makes a text appealing to children, for children love action. They like to be in on things that are happening. When there is a good plot, as well as a series of lively events, young audiences usually form a strong attachment to a book. Children become emotionally caught up in the prospect of change: change in the fortunes of the characters, sometimes fanciful and sometimes mildly realistic.

The fanciful story, more than any other type, illustrates the power of sheer inventiveness on the part of the writer. Here the elements of reality are juggled and recombined, imaginary beasts are invented, and supernatural powers are called into play. And whether the end result is nonsensical or adventurous, the child encounters a creative force which stretches his imagination and pleases him at the same time.

Theodor Seuss Geisel (1904–   )

A good fantasy achieves a delicate balance between invention and the restraints of logic. It can emerge only from a highly creative and uninhibited mind, but a skilled craftsman is required to control it, once conceived.

This happy combination of creativity and literary discipline was most notably expressed in the partnership of Theodor Seuss Geisel (better known simply as "Dr. Seuss") and his first wife, the late Helen Palmer Geisel. Whether written in prose or verse, the contribution Dr. Seuss has made to children's literature is unequaled in one particular genre: the fanciful picture-book story. His extraordinary imaginative capacity is seen in the plots he devises, the characters that inhabit his stories, and his use of language.

Dr. Seuss has acknowledged the assistance of his wife in maintaining high standards in both the plotting and the versification of his picture books. He told a journalist in 1957: "I keep losing my story line and Helen has to find it again. She's a fiend for story line."[1] She also criticized his rhymes until they were reworked dozens of times and finally perfected.

The majority of Seuss picture books are reminiscent of the moral tale, minus any strain of solemnity or didacticism. As Dr. Seuss has noted, "When we have a moral, we try to tell it sideways."[2] He works to keep his stories from ending in a maudlin way and feels that children should not be made "to feel you are trying to push something down their throats."[3] Even more important, the drama and characterization overshadow the moral to the point where children are not really conscious of it as part of their initial response. Thus the books are never a fraud, never beginning as entertainment but ending as admonition or reproach.

Horton Hears a Who (1954) is a moral tale based on the principle that "a person's a person, no matter how small," that no one is unimportant. Horton the elephant discovers a civilization of infinitesimal creatures ("Whos") residing upon a particle of dust, but his scoffing jungle friends plot to destroy the precious speck unless Horton can make his "Whos" heard or seen. It's a life-and-death kind of suspense that mounts as the Mayor of Whoville searches for another voice to swell his chorus of screaming "Whos."

"The Sneetches" (in *The Sneetches and Other Stories* [1961]) is another prime example and deals with the most crucial issue of our time: the foolishness of discrimination based on physical differences.

The Star-Belly and Plain-Belly Sneetches take turns, each group lording it over the other, until the story reaches this frenetic climax:

> All the rest of that day, on those wild screaming beaches,
> The Fix-it-up Chappie kept fixing up Sneetches.
> Off again! On again!
> In again! Out again!
> Through the machines they raced round and about again. . . .

Every detail of the story adds to our feeling of amusement and disgust toward creatures with such mindless prejudices. Finally the "Sneetches forgot about stars/ And whether they had one, or not, upon thars."

The creation of fanciful characters may be allied to Dr. Seuss's work as a cartoonist. However, on close examination we see that the real interest of his characters lies in the written descriptions rather than in the line portraits. He has never had the training of an artist, and the total visual impact of his books is one of sameness. He seems limited in what he can do with a line as a line (as an expressive graphic element) but not in the concoctions of his imagination.*

Verbal descriptions individualize his characters, as in *If I Ran the Circus* (1956):

> And now Here!
> In this cage
> Is a beast most ferocious
> Who's known far and wide
> As the Spotted Atrocious
> Who growls, howls and yowls
> The most bloodcurdling sounds
> And each tooth in his mouth
> Weighs at least 60 pounds
> And he chews up and eats with the greatest of ease
> Things like carpets and sidewalks and people and trees.

---

* One is tempted to speculate about what other illustrators might do with some of the Dr. Seuss stories after they come into the public domain. The prospect of new illustrations may seem shocking at first, but if the stories are judged by their intrinsic merits and the illustrations by their graphic quality, one can imagine an even greater pleasure for children if some of the tales were separated from their present cartoon illustrations, drawings that tend to be monotonous.

And from the same book:

> And you'll now meet the Foon! The Remarkable Foon
> Who eats sizzling hot pebbles that fall off the moon!
> And the reason he likes them red hot, it appears,
> Is he greatly enjoys blowing smoke from his ears.

Because of the many word inventions, intriguing characters, and fanciful plots, the Dr. Seuss books have become family traditions, already acclaimed by two generations. They will be read as long as children respond to humor, fantasy, and the sound of words.

Bill Peet (1915–   )

Bill Peet entered the field of writing for children with *Hubert's Hair-Raising Adventure* (1959), and he has been active ever since, both writing and illustrating. His talent as a writer is evident in all his children's books, but *Hubert* shows a quality of imagination that is rare. Like Dr. Seuss, Bill Peet illustrates in cartoon fashion, but the drawings are more complex than those of Dr. Seuss and are more expressive of characterization. He achieves a visual exaggeration that suitably emphasizes the ridiculous. Also like Dr. Seuss, he is a perfectionist when it comes to the rhythms and rhymes of a text in verse.

> Hubert the Lion was haughty and vain
> And especially proud of his elegant mane.
> But conceit of this sort isn't proper at all
> And Hubert the Lion was due for a fall.

When Hubert accidentally burns off his mane and is too ashamed and embarrassed to come out of hiding, the other animals try to think of some cure:

> "We could make," said the Zebra, "a wig out of weeds."
> "Or find," said the Rhino, "some hair-growing seeds."
> "With some cloth," said the Gnu, "and a needle and thread
> We could sew a big cap that would cover his head."

The elephant remembers that crocodile tears will produce the right effect, but after he goes to all the trouble to get them, he finds that they work *too* well. After the mane has grown to its proper length, it keeps on growing:

> It spiraled straight up in a great golden crest
> Then off to the south, to the north, east and west.
> It went swirling and circling and crawling and creeping
> All over his friends who were still soundly sleeping.

The ridiculous heights this story reaches would take too long to describe, but the humor is of the rowdy kind and highly pictorial. A riot ensues when the animals awake, their thrashing about naturally pulls Hubert's hair, they send for the Barber Baboon, and Hubert eventually emerges with a uniquely styled mane that makes him more smug and self-satisfied than ever.

Besides the ingenious idea of having a vain lion burn off his mane, this text has many little sidelights on human character and behavior. The cast includes not only the conceited Hubert, but also a gossip, a long-suffering friend, a pure rogue of a crocodile, and a whole group of animal acquaintances who are always ready with advice but never willing to do anything.

Descriptions are exceptionally vivid, but they never bog down the action. We learn just enough about each character to be sympathetic or, as with the crocodile, appropriately horrified. This villain becomes absolutely ecstatic over Hubert's misfortune:

> And then all at once he threw open his jaws
> And exploded with laughter in great loud guffaws.
> He held both his sides and he staggered around
> Until soon he was flopping all over the ground.

Bill Peet insists upon logic in every development of the plot, enabling the listener to thoroughly believe in the climax, one of the most boisterous slapstick scenes in all of picture-book literature.

Maurice Sendak (1928–   )

Maurice Sendak is an important picture-book writer, although he is also a popular illustrator and people usually think of him first as an artist. He has created some exceptional color illustrations for *The Moon Jumpers* (1959) and *Mr. Rabbit and the Lovely Present* (1962) and many amusing cartoon drawings. But it can nonetheless be argued that his texts may outlive some of his cartoon-style illustrations. *Pierre, a Cautionary Tale* (1962) is a case in point.

Sendak has a good sense of narrative form and pacing. And compared with many picture-book authors, he is meticulous with the rhythms in what he calls his "doggerel verse."[4] This term describes his style of writing accurately and yet it is somewhat misleading. It's not the verse per se that interests the listener; it's the drama and the rare ability Sendak has to express the child's sense of play, as well as his sense of humor and his exasperation in a world of authoritarian, giant-like adults. Doggerel plays a part in emphasizing the humor and is perhaps even necessary in a text which must be so exceedingly brief and still contain a discernible mood. It can be argued that the doggerel is more important to the spirit of this Sendak story than his repeated drawings of a Dennis-the-Menace-type child character.

Pierre resembles the cautionary tale parodies of Hilaire Belloc, but it more fully expresses the young child's habits and sense of play. The "bad boy" Pierre says "I don't care" until his parents are totally nonplused, but then he fails to modify this little joke when suddenly confronted by a hungry lion.

"I can eat you,
   don't you see?"
"I don't care!"
"And you will be
   inside of me."
"I don't care!"
"Then you'll never
   have to bother—"
"I don't care!"
"With a mother
   and a father."
"I don't care!"

The momentarily horrible consequences are described with dispatch and wit. Children respond with a playful mock fear, squirming and smiling simultaneously.

Where the Wild Things Are (1963) is also notable for its success with children as a form of play. Carolyn Horovitz has written about this aspect of the book and about the need to appreciate the paradoxes one finds in children's play. Leading up to her discussion of Sendak's story, she notes that when children play, "their violence never takes place between real antagonists, but always between those who are actually friends." She continues:

[Children's] "explorations" are always of the familiar, such as exploring under the table. The uncontrollable is not a subject for play. . . . Fiction, controlled by plot, can still involve children in a "play" sense, as long as the author is clearly writing fiction and thus inviting the child to participate. A remarkable example of a writer's ability to do this is Maurice Sendak's *Where the Wild Things Are*. He demonstrates a fine, sensitive awareness of release and control. Children's responses to this book are of such intense enjoyment that it is obviously one into which they can step freely, recognizing in the smiling wild things the paradox of play.[5]

Some critics stressed the fearsome aspect of the "wild things" when this book first appeared and warned parents against it; but the resolution of the "wild thing" fantasy happens so quickly in the story and so conclusively that such a warning seems absurd. The hero, Max, returns safe and sound to a warm supper in his own home, and his exceedingly brief encounter (the whole book takes not more than a few minutes to read) with imaginary, sharp-toothed beasts cannot be separated from the total context. Sendak himself has stressed the need for a fantasy to be thoroughly and satisfyingly resolved. He said, "Max . . . comes home. Mind you, he doesn't say, 'I'll never go there again. He *will* fantasize again, but the hope is that, like other children, he'll keep coming back to his mother.'"[6] Even the words used, such as "wild rumpus," have a comical rather than a serious sound and connotation. The style and tone of the story make even the youngest listener sure that this is a frolic from start to finish.

Jean de Brunhoff (1899–1937)

Babar the elephant, created by Jean de Brunhoff, first appeared in 1933 in *The Story of Babar, the Little Elephant*. This was five years before the first Dr. Seuss book, and except for the characters of Dr. Seuss, there are few inhabitants of picture books which have more loyal fans. This is due in part to the basic incongruity of an elephant driving a small car, bathing in a bathtub, doing setting-up exercises, wearing shoes with spats, and so on. It can perhaps be attributed also to the identification children feel when Babar engages in such childlike amusements as riding a department store elevator up and down ten times and being scolded: "Elevators are not toys." But in addition to these qualities, there is a fantastic mixture of animal and human traits in each character, and the author does not shy away from emotional kinds of experience. A great variety of life revolves around Babar as he grows up, grieves over the death of his mother, runs away to the city and then comes home again, is crowned king of the jungle, marries, goes on his honeymoon in a balloon, raises a family, and takes care of all his relatives and the citizens of his realm. Children find all the world in the Babar books; they serve children the way Jacques Barchilon says fairy tales serve them, as a "kind of apprenticeship to life."[7]

Besides the range of emotions, there is an overriding sense of warmth in the Babar stories which Bettina Hürlimann (*Three Centuries of Children's Books in Europe*) attributes to the circumstances of Jean de Brunhoff's life. He was forced by illness to reside in Switzerland and to correspond with his three young sons in France by mail. The correspondence consisted of Babar stories, and the story's chief character became an idealization of fatherhood. Babar, his children, and his friends are seen on the merry-go-round, at the theater, watching parades, eating cakes, going fishing, enjoying a happy companionship. Babar is "a French *père de famille* whose company it is always a pleasure to share."[8]

Something must be said about the style of the Babar stories also, for they are told in such a matter-of-fact tone that incidents sound credible and even serious. But at the same time, this appearance of nonchalance makes Babar very comical. Mrs. Hürlimann has noted that there is an "extreme directness of language, such as is usually only achieved by children. . . ."[9] This directness also has the effect of speeding up the action, and listeners are left a little bit breathless when the stories end.

The popularity of Babar can be explained in these terms, but the devotion that some children feel for him is still somewhat mystifying. For them his place is somehow never usurped by any other picture-book character.*

* After the first six Babar books, Jean de Brunhoff died and his eldest son took over the continuation of the series. Having been brought up on Babar stories, Laurent de Brunhoff was able to maintain, in some degree, the spirit of the original Babar. It should be noted that *The Travels of Babar* (1937), one of the original six, depicts Africans from a European colonialist viewpoint, with racist overtones. It is therefore the one objectionable title of the series and should be avoided.

Virginia Lee Burton (1909–1968)

When things such as snowplows, tugboats, or trains are personified in books for children, adult critics sometimes object. They find such extremes of anthropomorphism ludicrous. But since fascination with mechanical objects is basic in young children, a wholesale rejection of mechanical heroes is unrealistic and rather pointless. Handled adeptly, a character such as the snowplow Katy in *Katy and the Big Snow* (1943) by Virginia Lee Burton can be very real and exciting to the preschooler.

The author was a New England textile designer of some prominence, as well as the creator of stories and illustrations for children. The graphic design of her picture books is so integral to the whole story conception that it is difficult to conceive of texts and illustrations separately. In *Katy*, for example, each page engages the child in a kind of map-reading game, following the little trails of freshly plowed snow which zigzag, curve in and out, and become progressively more intricate.

The illustrations here are not particularly exciting in themselves, but as part of the idea of the story, they fulfill a narrative function. Katy is an ideal civil servant, a persevering snowplow with a large sense of duty and a kind of bravado about meeting challenges. In fact "the harder and tougher the job the better she liked it." The appeal of *Katy* probably lies in the heroics of the story more than in any other feature. Following a crippling blizzard, she plows pathways for the firemen, the postmen, the doctors, the police, and other townspeople. Although she begins to feel tired, "she wouldn't stop . . . not Katy." Each challenge is presented pictorially and described with parallel phrasing. A rhythm emerges, and children quickly memorize the dialogue:

> "Help," called out the postmaster. "Help us get the mail through."
> "Sure," said Katy. "Follow me."

The Little House (1942) is also an excellent example of the use of personification. Here Burton describes the life-cycle of a house—how it changes from a new, solidly built house in the country to a neglected, run-down slum house in the midst of high-rise buildings. This drastic change of fortune rights itself in the end with the "little house" being moved back to the country.

The drama inherent in this plot is felt by children, but they are also interested in the realistic detail as the countryside gradually evolves into a town and then a city. The first sign of change comes when the surveyors "[survey] a line in front of the Little House," and the author is very specific about each new development. The steam shovels "dug down three stories on one side and four stories on the other side. . . . They built up twenty-five stories on one side and thirty-five stories on the other."

The author had a thorough appreciation of the young child's delight in repetition, and her style capitalizes on this in *The Little House* as it does in *Katy*.

102

James Flora (1914–   )

Personified dolls and wind-up toys often have heroic roles in picture books, and one of the best examples is *Sherwood Walks Home* (1966) by James Flora. This story combines the pleasures of a cumulative form, a definite sense of character, slapstick humor, fantasy, and dramatic tension. Sherwood, the wind-up bear, has a clear and stubborn sense of identity as he repeatedly tells his adversaries: "I'm Robert's bear, and I must go home before my motor runs down." He is so frantic and so determined about this that he drags everything in his wake as he tries to reach Robert's house. (Thus the accumulation of incidents: a fish biting Sherwood's tail, a cat chasing the fish, a dog chasing the cat, and so on.) Processions of this kind are familiar in such folk stories as *The Old Woman and Her Pig* and *The Golden Goose,* but the slapstick aspect of Sherwood's situation is enlarged by the fact that he cannot turn corners; his mechanism makes him go in a straight line and hence he walks right along the bottom of a pond when he finds one in his path. (It's here that the fish catches him.)

The various lines of repetition are pleasing to young children in stories with this kind of form. But the excitement of meeting a crisis (suddenly being abandoned and homeless), the expression of obstinacy in Sherwood's remarks and also in his appearance, and the exuberant slapstick—these qualities enrich the story and heighten its appeal.

The charge of sentimentality can sometimes be made against stories featuring a child's favorite toy. But whereas sentimentality is a serious defect in all other genres of literature, in the well-conceived picture book it is seldom a valid ground for criticism. The picture-book text is so brief it *requires* the direct expression of emotion, the quick, conclusive climax. And this direct expression need not become cloying. Robert hugs his wind-up bear Sherwood, and then with one brief, amusing comment about Sherwood's sore tail, the story is over.

H. A. Rey (1898–   )

The series of stories beginning with *Curious George* (1941) by Margaret and Hans Rey depend upon a number of hazardous episodes, as much as upon character, for their success. George the curious monkey is not as engaging as Kipling's curious Elephant's Child in *Just So Stories* (1912); the plot and style of the George books are rather undeveloped. George simply works his way from one scrape to another. Still, George's well-meaning mischief is what attracts children. "Children identify with George," explains Mrs. Rey. "They want to paint a room they couldn't paint," or "clean the house with a water-shooting garden hose."[10]

Dramatic elements are very strong in the first book in the series and help to establish the appeal of the character. By the second page, George has been momentarily blinded by a big yellow hat over his eyes and caught and tied up in a sack. He nearly drowns; then he's chased and locked up in jail. He escapes by walking along some telephone wires. Finally we see him sailing through the air with a handful of balloons and descending onto the top of a traffic light.

The style of writing in the George books is too often similar to the style of a first-grade primer: The sentences are short, uniform, and monotonous. But the perilous exploits and the slapstick humor redeem these stories in the eyes of children, to the point that more than six million copies have been needed so far to supply the demand.[11]

The Ancient, Anonymous Storytellers

The value of folk literature is seldom questioned today, and when it is, the censors are usually those who have had meager exposure to it. The stories have been refined through countless years of telling; in fact, nothing else that we can offer children has stood such a test of time. The critical problems involve the comparison of editions and the suitability of the picture-book format for certain kinds of tales.

Illustrating individual folk tales gives them a literal dimension that must be viewed as a mixed blessing, even when the pictures are very good. Illustrations, by definition, depict content, and this is sometimes a problem in tales containing supernatural elements (trolls, elves, witches, and so on) and highly symbolic heroes and heroines. When outlined solely by the listener's imagination, characters of this sort retain more of their mysterious or ideal quality. The less literal delineation in a child's consciousness helps give such characters a needed otherworldly aspect, and their display of heroism and magical power is then all the more convincing.

For this reason we could say that the child's encounter with the story of *The Three Billy Goats Gruff* or *The Gunniwolf* should be unaccompanied by illustrations. *The Gunniwolf* in particular loses much of its power and charm when an illustrator attempts to envision and depict its characters. A gunniwolf must remain a figment of one's imagination because practically everything about him is indefinite. No one could even say what he looks like, although he seems wolf-like in the sense that *wolf* connotes something fearsome, something menacing.

Another reason for leaving this story unillustrated is that much of its attraction has to do with sound, and the sounds should remain the center of attention. There are fantasy, excitement, and an intermittent tension and relaxation as the gunniwolf chases the little girl and then promptly falls asleep when she begins to sing; more important are the song itself, the onomatopoeic sounds, and the parallel phrasing. Every time the gunniwolf catches up with the little girl, he says, "Sing that guten, sweeten song again," and she sings, "Kum-kwa, kum-kwa, kum-kwa;" then she runs pit-pat, pit-pat, pit-pat, and gets chased again, hunker-cha, hunker-cha, hunker-cha.

This story is available in picture book format, but the illustrations simply prove how unsatisfying the visualization of a myth can be. There is no great loss therefore when storytellers simply use the book—*The Gunniwolf* (1967)—to memorize the brief text.

Tikki Tikki Tembo (1968) retold by Arlene Mosel derives its humor and its drama from the complexity and euphony of a little boy's name. This tale could be skillfully and suitably illustrated by Blair Lent because, like many folk tales, it contains quite ordinary people and happenings. Its degree of exaggeration makes it a wonder tale (only a wondrously doting mother would name her first-born "Tikki tikki tembo – no sa rembo – chari bari ruchi – pip peri pembo," which means "the most wonderful thing in the whole wide world"). However, the story contains no magic and the characters are not completely idealized. This kind of tale lends itself to graphic depiction as well as any other picture-book story. It can be full of rhythm and pattern and verbal nonsense and at the same time be portrayed graphically by an artist. Similarly, the sense of wonder is not seriously lessened by showing what the numskull characters do in *Nail Soup* (1964) or *Mommy, Buy Me a China Doll* (1966), both illustrated by Margot Zemach. However, it is important that tales like this be read or spoken out loud, even when accompanied by illustrations. Like poems, their essential charm depends upon sound.

Tales with animal protagonists lend themselves to picture-book treatment when the animals are realistic in appearance, if not in behavior. For example, Hans Fischer's illustrated version of *The Traveling Musicians* (1955) is a distinguished rendition, with none of the mystical features weakened by visualization.

On the other hand, for the first exposure to such tales as *Cinderella, The Sleeping Beauty,* or *Snow White and Rose Red* (where a kind of ideal woman is portrayed), purely oral presentations are best. Afterwards the beautiful graphic renditions can be introduced, as, for example, those by Marcia Brown, Felix Hoffmann, and Adrienne Adams.

The appeal of the folk tale can be tested with each new generation of children, and with sure results. These tales contain the best themes, humor, drama, rhythm, imagery, and imaginative content to be found in children's books. But there are many different editions or retellings of the most popular tales, and some of these are so poor that none of the appealing qualities of the ancient versions remain. For example, in the "Holly Story Library" editions (published by World Publishing Company), the most pleasing literary features have been removed. The structural economy, the aural patterns, the colloquialisms, the balanced rise and fall of the fortunes of antagonist and protagonist, the symbolic quality of the characters, the dramatic strength and intensity, the cause-and-effect relationships—all these elements have been seriously weakened. Nothing is left but a few remnants of the original plot, presented in a dull, verbose style. Publishers who treat folk tales in this manner make no announcement on the title page or elsewhere in the book warning the buyer about the liberties taken. But if readers will become familiar with versions of tales compiled by such folklorists and writers as the Brothers Grimm, Charles Perrault, Peter Asbjørnsen, Joseph Jacobs, Andrew Lang, Harold Courlander, and Ruth Manning-Sanders, they will be able to recognize good and bad editions with just a quick scanning of the texts.

Conclusion

Centuries of experience have proved the appeal of folk narratives; and, in the case of original modern tales such as *Babar, Curious George,* and the Dr.

Seuss stories, several generations have had the opportunity to show their approval. This tells the critic something about the essential features of a good picture-book narrative. Summarized briefly, its elements can be seen in relation to two other arts, the novel and the dance. As book editor Jean Karl has noted, "The true picture-book story, no matter how simple, is often of really heroic scope. It can be said to be a small novel. . . ."[12] In other words, a lot goes on in the picture-book narrative: There are many changes of scene, and the action affects the chief character significantly (often involving his very survival). At the same time, with respect to form, the picture-book text is patterned and symmetrical. Geoffrey Trease has made a comparison between the dance, symphonic composition, and the folk tale, calling attention to the rhythmic design and movement in all three.[13] Many of the best picture-book texts resemble these old tales with repeated chants and narrative patterns.

8

Specialized Texts

IN JUDGING a specialized type of picture-book text, criteria must be used which are quite distinct from the criteria used for narrative fiction. The purpose of the text is not to tell a story, but, in some imaginative way, to inform the child about his world or meet some of his various needs. For example, there are bedtime books created for the sole purpose of getting the child in the mood for sleep. There are nursery chronicles, miniature travelogues and appreciations of nature, alphabet and counting books, concept books, books serving as verbal and visual games, and so on. Any number of groupings and labels come to mind, and their usefulness is simply to aid the critic in reaching a fair judgment by applying the criteria that fit each group.

A pragmatic approach is required in judging these texts because they succeed when their limited purpose is achieved. If the book is basically a type of game rather than a story, the child must be capable of playing it successfully. An adult cannot judge the book by his own reaction; he can best judge it in the company of young children at the suitable age level, observing the children's responses and joining them in the spirit of play.

With a nursery chronicle (a book simply describing household events in a young child's experience), the critic in the company of a child can see whether or not the book is succeeding with its intended audience, whether or not the child is deeply involved in identifying with a book character who appears to be almost like himself. A child will often attach his own name to the central character and designate the other family characters in the book as the members of his own family. Another clue to his response is the number of times he wants to return to the book.

Some of the criteria for fiction cannot be applied to a book like this, for it usually has no plot at all, no dramatic situation or climax, and no unique sense of character. It must be judged in relation to what it is, and not on the basis of what it is not even intended to be.

Humor and style will enhance any text, even one with the limited purpose of presenting the alphabet or illuminating a simple concept. In many of the best specialized texts, humor plays a major part in the book's appeal. In fact, if the book is enjoyed by children beyond the age of about four years, it is probably because of humorous elements or distinguished graphic art which go beyond the basic intentions of the text.

As a general rule it can also be said that the quality of the illustrations is doubly important in specialized picture books because the verbal and imaginative content is so slight. In the sampling of recommended books in this chapter, illustrations range from competent cartoons to exceptional examples of design, originality, and craftsmanship.

ABC and Counting Books

ABC and counting books are not recent innovations in picture-book literature. The alphabet text "A Was an Apple Pie" was referred to in 1671 as if commonly known in England, and Kate Greenaway added further to its popularity when she used it as a picture-book text in 1886.[1]

Maurice Sendak adds nonsensical incongruities and alliteration to his presentation of the alphabet in *Alligators All Around* (1962) (part of the four-volume set called "The Nutshell Library"). He has his alligators doing such unlikely things as "B—bursting balloons. . ." or "G—getting giggles. . ." or "O—ordering oatmeal. . ." or "P—pushing people. . . ."

An edition of *Peter Piper's Alphabet* (1959) with illustrations by Marcia Brown was a welcome addition to alphabet literature. These alliterative jingles were published originally in London and then in 1830 in Massachusetts.[2] Imagery, slapstick humor, and the wildest kind of word play are characteristic of this text. The verbal gymnastics delight children as they repeat not only the "Peter Piper picked a peck of pickled peppers" verse, but also "Enoch Elkrig ate an empty Eggshell," and

> Quixote Quicksight quizzed a queerish Quidbox;
> Did Quixote Quicksight quiz a queerish Quidbox?
> If Quixote Quicksight quizzed a queerish Quidbox,
> Where's the queerish Quidbox Quixote Quicksight quizzed?

And so on for each letter.

A simple but dynamically illustrated counting book by Fritz Eichenberg, *Dancing in the Moon* (1956), presents the numbers up to twenty and uses rhymes and nonsense images. For example, Eichenberg depicts "one raccoon dancing in the moon," and "eight llamas wearing pajamas."

Visual and Verbal Games

Some picture-book texts manage to get along without words entirely. In *The Adventures of Paddy Pork* (1968) by John S. Goodall, a small melodrama must be traced by the child through his "reading" of the illustrations. The technique needed to play this game is visual, but the book's quality rests not with the illustrations alone, but with the ease in perceiving the action of the drama, the excitement of the drama, and the overall idea of a story told without words.

Snail, Where Are You? (1962) by Tomi Ungerer has no written text until the last two pages where the question in the title is answered and the snail says, "Here I am." Until this last page, the book consists of delightful pictures in which the motif of a snail's shell is employed on other objects: the peg end of a violin, the tip of an old-fashioned ice skate, the tail of a pig, and so forth. This book can be judged by its success as a game (the snail design is easy for children to discover) and by its originality of concept (the ingenious placement and treatment of the visual motif). *Look What I Can Do* (1971) by Jose Aruego has no text other than the words in the title and the response: "I can do it too." For the viewer the challenge is to trace visually the parallel actions of two animal characters who become engaged in a humorously exhausting game of follow-the-leader across mountains, rivers, and valleys.

Some picture books are guessing games with various kinds of questions for the child to answer. One of the most original is Sesyle Joslin's *What Do You Say, Dear? or a handbook of etiquette for young ladies and gentlemen to be used as a guide for everyday social behavior* (1958). After a scene or situation has been described by the author, the question "What do you say, dear?" is asked and the answer is obvious enough for the child to guess before the page is turned. For example, a typical page reads:

> You have gone downtown to do some shopping.
> You are walking backwards, because sometimes
> you like to, and you bump into a crocodile.
> What do you say, dear?

On the following page the answer, "Excuse me!" is given, but the child usually guesses it immediately, and this challenge, as well as participation in the dialogue, pleases him.

This text is notable also for its accuracy in depicting the young child's nature, his delight in topsy-turvies (walking backwards), in slapstick, and in mythical and prehistoric beasts.

Nursery Chronicles

The typical nursery chronicle depicts average children during the course of an average day or week. The setting is usually the child's home or nursery school. This kind of text helps the child project himself into familiar scenes and enjoy the process of recognition, as well as the warmth and security associated with the scenes.

Lucy and Tom's Day (1960) by Shirley Hughes is an unpretentious chronicle and avoids the sentimentality that sometimes finds its way into books about a preschooler's daily life. Although Lucy and Tom are English and the neighborhood scenes slightly different from those of America, there are dozens of familiar objects that a child can identify on each page. The text is simply a caption for each picture, yet it is apt and childlike: "Lucy is scraping the last bit of cereal out of her bowl. Tom has finished his and is waving his spoon for some more."

In using books like this, one finds that half the fun is the child's excitement about his own family and his eagerness to talk about it. In fact story hours using this kind of book end up being a continuous series of conversations with the audience, and sometimes the book is forgotten altogether.

Concept Books

The concept book attempts to illumine some relationship between obects or ideas, or categorize the likenesses and differences of things. Colors, shapes, softness and hardness, distance, speed—these are common topics in picture books, and there are also such abstract subjects as friendship, love, privacy. Clarity is a requisite in these books, especially in those designed with a rather explicit educational purpose, but there is also room for originality in treatment and for humor and style.

Classifying concepts and feelings for a child audience is apparently not so easy as it appears, for authors often lapse into an inconsistent treatment of their subjects. This could be partially due to efforts to rhyme the text, as in *A Kiss Is Round* (1954) by Blossom Budney. In an otherwise pleasing and useful book, the verses about round objects are suddenly interrupted by this confusing, paradoxical idea:

> A balloon and a bubble are round with air
> But a walk-aROUND the block is SQUARE.

But if the search for a rhyme does not obscure the concept, rhymes are a strong asset, adding a needed liveliness. Without rhymes, rhythms, poetic cadence, or distinguished illustrations, a concept book runs the risk of dullness. Many now on the market would not find an audience if it were not for the situations in which children are, in every sense, a captive audience.

The most common redeeming factor in concept books is imaginative and skillful illustration. Many books appear to have been conceived as vehicles for an artist. But there are instances in which the text can be recommended as well; for example, *The Wing on a Flea* (1961) by Ed Emberley. This book is subtitled *A Book About Shapes,* and for such a talented designer as Emberley, this subject matter is ideal. His drawings are a mass of fragile, whimsical lines and details, and he has brightly colored blocks for the triangle, rectangle, and circle shapes. His verses have an easy lilt:

> A triangle is
> The wing on a flea,

And the beak on a bird,
If you'll just look and see.

Each verse in the text is closely associated with an illustration, and the total effect on the child is like that of a game as he locates the shapes which have been ingeniously placed in the pictures (the beak on the bird, the tail of the fish, the ice-cream cone, and so on).

A Little House of Your Own (1955), written by Beatrice Schenk de Regniers and illustrated by Irene Haas, treats in considerable detail the subject of privacy. It is also full of playtime suggestions, such as using a blanket on the clothesline to make a tent, or a large umbrella as a private hideaway. Impressing the reader with the joys of privacy is the book's main purpose, but the whimsical treatment gives it a special dimension. There is also a brief word about etiquette for those who may be outside "the little house":

If somebody *has* to bother you—
if your mother has to tell you to
get ready for dinner because it is
dinnertime—
then she should be very polite.

She should walk softly
and knock gently at the door
of your little house and she
should speak quietly and tell
you, "Pretty soon it will be time to
leave your little house and get
ready for dinner."

Miniature Travelogues

Many picture books are designed to give young children a glimpse of a foreign country, but the texts are not usually written as straight nonfiction. As often happens in documentary films, a slight fictional story is the framework for the text, while the foreign geography and customs are the real interests of author and artist.

One prevailing characteristic of these picture-book "documentaries" is a sense of atmosphere, of vibrant local color. Remote settings provide the climate of adventure even when dramatic incident is lacking, and these mysterious settings can stir the imagination. A strong writer will distinguish his characters also and bring a dramatic climax to the story, but in most miniature travelogues the reader finds little in the way of characterization or plot. The author simply wants to present a panorama of foreign life.

A Wish for Little Sister (1960) by Jacqueline Ayer is a good example. The author (who is also the illustrator) depicts scenes in Thailand, and although the story line deals with the ever-popular subject of birthdays, it is the country itself which is most intriguing. The author shows the heroine looking for a suitable

111

birthday wish and asking weavers, merchants of silk, and the candy vendor for suggestions. Through their replies various segments of Thai culture are presented. One cousin, for example, wishes she could become a royal court dancer, and this gives Ayer the opportunity to show the dancers' costumes.

The author is careful not to burden her fragile story with elaborate or redundant comment. It unfolds with artful simplicity and directness, Thailand itself remaining the center of interest.

Books About Nature

Books dealing with the weather, the seasons, and the lives of animals and insects are numerous in picture-book literature and range all the way from life-cycle stories to poetic frolics about rain and snow. Some of these books could be called science books, but more often they are impressionistic descriptions designed to sharpen the child's senses and general level of awareness.

The Honeybees (1967) by Franklin Russell, with pictures by Colette Portal is a poetic attempt to relate the life-cycle of a honeybee. The sound of the bees is described as "a murmur, a buzz, a groan of wings in the wind . . . ," and the flowers where they hunt form "jungles of color."

Betty Miles evokes the spirit of summertime and wintertime in her books *A Day of Summer* (1960) and *A Day of Winter* (1961). (Only these two, in the series about the seasons, contain the distinguished illustrations of Remy Charlip.) The author uses a free-verse form:

> See the late winter sun
> Blaze in cold sky.
> See sparkles of color
> On sharp, crusted snow.
> Watch blue shadows spreading
> On houses and trees.
> See small, huddled shadows
> of faraway children,
> Pulling sleds home.

Looking, listening, tasting, smelling, and feeling the seasons is the approach in both books, and the language and imagery can be easily understood by the youngest child.

Books which place their emphasis on something besides a narrative line could be cited by the hundreds. But it is perhaps enough to mention one more example, Karla Kuskin's *James and the Rain* (1957). All the excitement and giddy pleasure that rainy days produce in young children can be found here, and the jingling text makes it difficult for anyone to escape the fever.

> James had a very yellow coat
> That buttoned to his chin
> He had a pair of rubber boots

112

To tuck his trousers in
He took a big umbrella
From the big umbrella stand
He buttoned up his yellow coat
And looked extremely grand
He opened his umbrella
With the handle made of cane
He pulled his yellow hat down tight
And stepped into the rain.

9
The Caldecott Award

ANYONE searching for good picture books can turn to several annual lists to help him. The New York *Times,* in its fall Children's Book Section, lists the ten best illustrated books of the year and includes a sample illustration from each. The majority of books on this list are picture books. The *Horn Book Magazine* has an annual "Fanfare Honor List," and it always includes a picture-book section. By reading the annotations on the American Library Association's annual "Notable Books" list (the children's list), the reader can locate the "notable" picture books. Moreover, the American Institute of Graphic Arts exhibits from time to time a collection of well-designed and well-printed children's books and issues a catalogue listing them.*

However, one accolade for picture books influences the public above all others: the annual Caldecott award, which is given to an American illustrator or one residing in the United States. The public receives so little information and guidance about children's books through the mass media that teachers and parents will snatch up any book mentioned favorably in the press. The Caldecott and Newbery prize books are often the sole titles mentioned in publications which reach the general public. (The Newbery prize is awarded to the author of the most distinguished contribution to American literature for children.) To most people, the Caldecott award serves as an unquestioned stamp of quality. Bookstores and libraries display the winning books and the runners-up prominently when the award is announced, the publishers often go back to press for additional copies, parents purchase the books as special visual treats for their children, and pre-school and elementary school teachers use them without reservation. Even more

* The *Horn Book Magazine* is especially valuable for its commentaries and reviews, but its coverage is much more complete for texts than for illustrations. Generally speaking, critics from the field of graphic art have yet to be tapped for the extensive contribution they could make to children's book criticism.

important, the teachers of teachers in colleges and universities often refer to these picture books and to no others as the chief standard-bearers.

The Caldecott award was established by the American Library Association (ALA) in 1938 for "the artist of the most distinguished American picture book for children." Frederic Melcher, then principal editor of *Publishers Weekly* and the donor of the Newbery Medal, donated the Caldecott Medal and chose its name. Both awards were for the purpose of encouraging high standards in books for children, and it is generally assumed that this purpose is being achieved. Irene Smith writes, in *A History of the Newbery and Caldecott Medals*, that "the award books . . . provide a regularly renewed, firm, accessible guide for measuring literary and artistic endeavor. Most of them are very good examples, in theory of course our best examples, of standards the critics uphold. They are ideals demonstrated."[1]

A comparison of the Caldecott winners, the runners-up, and those books which did not even place in the runner-up category, reveals that the ideals have not been demonstrated as often as one would hope. Here are some of the notable books left out altogether in the last eighteen years:

Andy Says . . . Bonjour! illustrated by Chris Jenkyns;
    text by Pat Diska (1954)
Beasts from a Brush written and illustrated by
    Juliet Kepes (1955)
I Know a Lot of Things illustrated by Paul Rand;
    text by Ann Rand (1956)
The Dead Bird illustrated by Remy Charlip; text by
    Margaret Wise Brown (1958)
The Emperor and the Nightingale illustrated by Bill Sokol;
    text by Hans Christian Andersen (1959)
The Snow and the Sun re-told and illustrated by
    Antonio Frasconi (1961)
Madeline in London written and illustrated by
    Ludwig Bemelmans (1961)
Henri's Walk to Paris illustrated by Saul Bass;
    text by Leonore Klein (1962)
The Tomato Patch written and illustrated by
    William Wondriska (1964)
Mazel and Shlimazel; or The Milk of a Lioness
    illustrated by Margot Zemach; text by Isaac Bashevis Singer (1967)
Chinese Mother Goose Rhymes illustrated by
    Ed Young; text by Robert Wyndham (1968)
A Firefly Named Torchy written and illustrated by
    Bernard Waber (1970)
The Winter Picnic illustrated by Deborah Ray;
    text by Robert Welber (1970)

The illustrators of these books have interpreted and artistically extended

116

the different texts in a highly personal manner, with bold, original designs and unique style. It seems a pity that not one of them was selected.

Of the sixty-eight different titles listed as winners or runners-up during the first fourteen years of the prize, only about a dozen are noteworthy for both craftsmanship and originality of style. The following six artists placed only as runners-up: Boris Artzybasheff (*The Seven Simeons*, 1937); James Daugherty (*Andy and the Lion*, 1938); Ludwig Bemelmans (*Madeline*, 1939); Georges Schreiber (*Bambino the Clown*, 1947); Marcia Brown (*Henry—Fisherman*, 1949); and Nicholas Mordvinoff (*The Two Reds*, 1950).

During the last two decades there has been a slight improvement. Mordvinoff, Bemelmans, Brown, and Sidjakov have received the top prize. Leo Lionni and Taro Yashima have been among the runners-up, Lionni three times and Yashima three times.

The reason for the recurrent discrepancy between theory and practice is not too difficult to discover. The ALA resolution which set up the Caldecott award provided that "members of the Newbery Medal Committee will serve as judges."[2] This means that the jury is composed of persons knowledgeable about written texts (for the Newbery prize is concerned solely with written texts). At no point is experience in the field of art even mentioned as a prerequisite for the judges. This is the major problem in the Caldecott award system: no definite qualifications in art are required for the committee members, and consultants from the field of the visual arts are not even brought in as advisers.* Only on rare occasions are the committee members who are best qualified to judge a piece of writing equally well qualified to judge a work of graphic art. The education of librarians is very diverse and would only coincidentally include both a literary and a visual arts background. For this reason, probably the quickest way to raise the artistic level of the prize winners would be to bring in resource people from the field of art criticism. Art critics and historians, museum personnel or professors of graphic art might work with the committee during its preliminary studies of the leading nominees.

If such experts screened out those books which fall below a certain level, this would spare both the library world and the art world the embarrassment of a poorly conceived and designed award-winner. Graphic art critics would not always agree among themselves as to which book is best, but they would quickly reach a consensus on the clearly inferior works and put them out of the running.

Frederic Melcher wrote that "the responsibility for the award leads librarians to give more careful study to the new books."[3] This is one laudable aspect of the present award system, and its importance needs to be assessed. Irene

---

*The Newbery-Caldecott committee is composed of twenty-three people, all members of the Children's Services Division (CSD) of ALA. Four are officers of CSD; five are members of the Book Evaluation Committee, chosen by the CSD president; six are directly appointed by the CSD president; and eight are elected from a slate of sixteen at the annual CSD elections. Although any member of CSD may submit a nomination for a book to receive the Newbery or Caldecott award, final selection rests with this rather cumbersome committee.

Smith is even more emphatic in claiming that the award is an impetus to the librarian's education. She writes:

> No one has sufficiently emphasized the keen edge of professional interest which the Newbery and Caldecott Medals provide for those whose work is connected with children's books. They are a spur to the eternal search for quality, and a boon to the spirit of the children's librarian. . . . A day comes when every children's librarian passes judgment, either with a ballot, or perhaps only in her own mind. The incentive to do so, which stems from these Medals, makes them an important, pleasure-giving, vitalizing influence.[4]

Self-education for librarians is beneficial, but this should be seriously weighed against the damage that results if poorly qualified judges make the selection. The influence on the public is too far-reaching to permit the mere "vitalizing influence" for librarians to remain the central feature of the process.[*]

In 1946 Mr. Melcher outlined the benefits to writers, illustrators and publishers: "The winners of these Medals find tens of thousands of new readers. The honor is printed to their credit for years to come. Every new book of theirs has the better chance for a hearing."[5] The central problem is to balance immediate benefits to the professionals with those related to the whole artistic development of children's literature. Only a renewed commitment to prize-winners as models of visual excellence can produce a long-range upward trend. In fact, badly chosen award books can have a negative influence on standards and mislead the public.

It has sometimes been suggested that no awards be given when the nominees are lacking in a notable degree of originality and good craftsmanship, when they fail to serve as genuine visual models for the public. In 1948 the chairman of the Awards Committee wrote this reply to queries from her committee about the possibility of waiving the prize: "To omit an award is rather a difficult thing to do. In the first place only one good book out of approximately seven hundred is needed and that is likely to turn up when the sifting begins."[6] No reason is given here as to why the waiving of the prize would be difficult, and the conclusion that something will just "turn up" suggests a lack of commitment. Without the possibility of waiving the award in bad years, the credibility of the prize will remain in serious doubt to people in the arts.

Questions of definition as well as questions of art arise in the process of selecting a Caldecott winner. For example, the length and quality of a book's text receives considerable attention, for there has not yet been a definition of *picture*

---

[*] The need to educate librarians in the area of book illustration is not reduced by involving art critics in the award process. The American Library Association could reasonably initiate frequent conferences on picture books and create a graphic arts division on its staff for the children's literature magazine *Top of the News*. Whatever aids of this sort might be instituted, the important thing would be to create encounters between the professional world of art criticism and the world of children's literature.

book which all committee members will accept. Some judges will reject a book because the text is too long and the illustrations too sparse. Their definition of picture book is limited to those publications in which every detail of a text is shown visually. In the past some books have won the prize despite this objection, but the point is still being argued, and the narrowest definition is still held by some librarians.

Mr. Melcher was queried about the distinction between an illustrated book and a picture book and stated simply that "the initiative and dominant feature must be the work of the artist."[7] How dominant? is a question that takes up the time of judges and needs to be settled in advance.

The quality of the text is also a topic for debate. In the beginning Mr. Melcher offered only this general directive: "We suggest that the books be judged by the pictures but that the text should be worthy of the pictures."[8] This can be interpreted in different ways. Some Caldecott judges feel that the text must be a distinguished example of picture-book writing. Others feel that it need be just good enough to warrant purchase of the book by a library, that it be basically unobjectionable as an added title.

Since the picture book has several distinct parts, every critic must deal with them in some sequence, however often he claims to be interested only in the whole. Either he considers the text first, or the illustrations, or the typography, layout, and binding, or what he considers to be the mood of the text and whether or not the illustrations are in the same spirit. But since the Caldecott award is given to an illustrator, the judge's obligation is surely to consider illustrations first, and then see whether or not the other ingredients fall below a desired level. Any part of the book could disqualify the whole if it is so poor as to totally distract the reader.

This confusion over the importance of the text, when the prize is given to honor the illustrator, has led to some puzzling decisions; for example, the inclusion in the runner-up category of Dr. Seuss, an imaginative and skillful writer, but an illustrator whose cartoon drawings do not compare with what a real artist can create with line, color, shape, and texture. As Dr. Seuss himself has said: "I just never learned to draw."[9]*

The Caldecott prize needs, first of all, to have meaning as an art prize, for visual content is a predominant feature of nearly all the books a child encounters during his first seven or eight years of life. Artist Nicholas Mordvinoff writes:

> Book illustration stands somewhere between pure art and commercial art— in essence attached to the former, but in the production end of it, attached to the latter, book-making being a form of mass production. It would be

---

* Although Dr. Seuss does not fit the qualifications for a Caldecott winner, he is ideally qualified for the Laura Ingalls Wilder Award. It is hard to fathom why he has not received this prize, awarded every five years in recognition of an author or illustrator whose books, published in the United States, have over a period of years made a substantial and lasting contribution to literature for children. The American Library Association makes this award.

ideal if fine artistic achievement could find its place in the domain of mass production.[10]

This is precisely the goal implied in the Caldecott award: the encouragement of picture books related, in essence, to pure art.

10

The Child,
the Librarian,
and the Critic

I N THE CHILDREN's book market, alas, the buyer is not the consumer."[1] These words of despair by Margot Hentoff in *The New York Review of Books* are perfectly true. However, the problem is much reduced if the buyer is very close to the consumer, and this is why certain obligations must be accepted by librarians and critics.

The book reviewer too often sends forth his advice to the world with opinions based upon a sampling of one or two children. He observes the reading or listening habits of a child in his immediate family or among his acquaintances and then generalizes from this basis. Such a small sample is hardly reliable.

Librarians, if they are serving their communities well, do not make this mistake. The children's librarian is constantly in touch with hundreds of children, and if he utilizes the opportunities to know them well, he should be a good judge of their capacities and interests. His most valuable opportunity is in his role as their chief storyteller. The children's librarian is not really close to children as consumers of literature and art if he confines his work to organizing a collection, rushing about giving advice, or checking books out over a counter. He must see and feel how audiences respond to specific books in the library story hours, at Head Start story hours, at recreation centers, in the parks, in the classrooms of neighborhood schools. He must accept this role of performer in order to achieve his other goals—choosing books wisely, guiding the public, and helping the development of children's literature through his work as a book critic.

At present, children's literature suffers from the results of this paradox: Literary critics and art critics don't find the time and opportunity to work as librarians (as storytellers for vast numbers of children), and librarians don't find the time and necessary solitude for writing literary and art criticism. Ideally, the two activities should support each other in a complementary relationship.

It is harder than some adults realize to retain a sense of the child's experience of life. We get glimpses of the fact that this life is full of fantasy, anxiety, slapstick humor, superstition, mysteries of all sorts, and even grandiose dreams of power (such as the hero, Max, displays in *Where the Wild Things Are*).[2] James Higgins describes the child's experience in *Beyond Words: Mystical Fancy in Children's Literature:*

> The child's world is filled with solemn rites, incantations, and talismans. And why? Because these are all ingredients of *story*, and the child's world, one should remember, is very much closer to the story world than it is to the world of science.[3]

On the visual side, children delight in skillful and playful manipulations of color, line, shape, and pattern. The critic Clive Bell observed that "only artists and . . . children feel the significance of form so acutely that they know how things look. They see, because they see emotionally; and no one forgets the things that have moved them."[4] But we gradually lose touch with this unique experience of childhood unless we put ourselves in the right place to observe it. For the librarian as book critic this means chiefly the story hour.

When children are fully involved with a story they laugh, hold their breath, change positions, touch their neighbors, look positively frozen with stillness and react in similar visible ways. The adult must be an intimate part of all this in order to develop his awareness of books which are "good" for a child, books "which capture a child because they are saying something significant to him."[5]

After countless story hours, a librarian gains some confidence in generalizing about the ingredients of good children's stories and illustrations, but he must still return repeatedly to experiences with the real audience and verify his assumptions. This activity is one of the things which qualify a librarian to work as a critic or selector of books. His experience backs him up as he gives a reasoned account of how children can be expected to respond to a book and why. He is not forgetful of the interdependence and associations of all the parts of a picture book: the illustrations, the text, and the design of the whole book as a three-dimensional object. The examination of separate features is simply a method for fully illuminating the whole, balancing the strengths and weaknesses in the hope that the strengths will win, will outweigh any deficiencies.

Experiences with many children and many books lead the critic to a degree of caution in saying in advance what the good picture book will be like. He cannot predict what will turn up entirely outside the typical narrative patterns and the previous range of visual expression. For example, who could have anticipated

What Do You Say, Dear? and the triumph it would be in story hours? Or the pleasure children derive from bird forms that slide off the pages in Lionni's *Inch by Inch?* Henry James made this point about the novel, and it applies to books for children as well:

> . . . the good health of an art which undertakes so immediately to reproduce life must demand that it be perfectly free. It lives upon exercise, and the very meaning of exercise is freedom. The only obligation to which in advance we may hold a novel, without incurring the accusation of being arbitrary, is that it be interesting.[6]

The good critic also keeps in mind the fact that his role is different from that of the creative artist. He works "after the fact," whereas the creative artist is denied this luxury. To create an original work that will successfully communicate with children is a completely new and risky venture for the creator. He has no clear-cut guidelines except the artistic demands of his art form, the high level of performance that work in the fine arts implies.

The artist Nicholas Sidjakov tells about discovering this fact during a conversation with his son. He says the child was tired of hearing such remarks as "When you grow up you can do this . . . ," and "When you grow up you can do that . . . ," and with a child's logic the boy finally retorted, "When I grow up and you will be a little boy . . ." Sidjakov goes on to explain:

> It took me a while to realize that it seemed quite probable to him that as some people are growing taller, others must be getting shorter—to keep things balanced, I suppose. Now this type of reasoning would seem very valid to us, if we could forget everything we know or have experienced. . . . I realized how vain an attempt to foresee a child's reactions would be. . . . I forgot all about children while trying to do the best I could and something I would be satisfied with, and then, hoping for the best, submitted the final drawings to my son and his friends for approval. This method proved to be satisfactory to all parties. . . .[7]

As a creative illustrator Sidjakov could not generalize about children's books the way the critic does because, in the process, he would stifle his originality. He would become preoccupied with earlier successful models and be driven to an unconscious urge to imitate. In this way his primary gift to children—originality of thought and perception—would be lost.

The critic does not follow the creative path, but his task is vital to the long-term development of an art. Speaking about literature specifically, Henry Seidel Canby stated:

> Unless there is somewhere an intelligent critical attitude against which a writer can measure himself, where he can get punches and return them, . . . one of the chief requirements for good literature is wanting.[8]

Over the past fifty years, distinguished picture books have been gradually accumulating. If relationships are close between children, librarians, critics, and the public in general, these books will continue to be valued, and new books will meet the challenge of comparison with them. With the thoughtful, candid support of critics and librarians, the artist can joyfully do his work for children, for that "vast reservoir of impressionists" Ludwig Bemelmans discovered, who are "very clear-eyed and capable of enthusiasm."[9]

Picture Books Mentioned in This Study

All these books are recommended, some primarily for their texts (when discussed under the headings Literary Elements, Outstanding Narrative Writers, or Specialized Texts) and others primarily for illustrations. Even those titles recommended with some reservations in Chapter 5, Book Design, are better than the average picture book with respect to illustrations.

Adams, Adrienne, illustrator. *See* Grimm, Jacob and Grimm, Wilhelm, *The Shoemaker and the Elves;* Grimm, Jacob and Grimm, Wilhelm, *Snow White and Rose Red.*

Akaba, Suekichi, illustrator. *See* Otsuka, Yuzo.

Andersen, Hans Christian. *The Emperor and the Nightingale.* Pantheon, 1959. Illustrated by Bill Sokol.

——. *The Steadfast Tin Soldier.* Scribner's, 1953. Illustrated by Marcia Brown.

Artzybasheff, Boris, author-illustrator. *The Seven Simeons.* Viking, 1937.

Aruego, Jose, author-illustrator. *Look What I Can Do.* Scribner's, 1971.

Asbjörnsen, Peter and Moe, Jörgen. *The Three Billy Goats Gruff.* Harcourt, 1957. Illustrated by Marcia Brown.

Ayer, Jacqueline, author-illustrator. *A Wish for Little Sister.* Harcourt, 1960.

Baker, Laura Nelson. *The Friendly Beasts.* Parnassus, 1957. Illustrated by Nicolas Sidjakov.

Balet, Jan, author-illustrator. *Joanjo: A Portuguese Tale.* Delacorte, 1967.

Bass, Saul, illustrator. *See* Klein, Leonore.

Baumann, Hans. *Fenny, the Desert Fox.* Pantheon, 1970. Illustrated by Eleonore Schmid.

Bemelmans, Ludwig, author-illustrator. *Madeline.* Viking, 1939.

——. *Madeline in London.* Viking, 1961.

——. *Madeline's Rescue.* Viking, 1953.

Birnbaum, Abe, author-illustrator. *Green Eyes.* Capitol, 1953.

Bobri, Vladimir, illustrator. *See* Budney, Blossom.

Brooke, Leslie, author-illustrator. *The Golden Goose.* Warne, 1905.

——. *Johnny Crow's Garden.* Warne, 1903.

Brown, Marcia, author-illustrator. *Henry—Fisherman.* Scribner's, 1949.

——. *Once a Mouse.* Scribner's, 1961.

——, illustrator. *See* Andersen, Hans Christian, *The Steadfast Tin Soldier;* Asbjörnsen, Peter C. and Moe, Jörgen; Perrault, Charles, *Cinderella;* Perrault, Charles, *Puss-in-Boots; Peter Piper's Alphabet.*

Brown, Margaret Wise. *The Dead Bird.* Scott, 1958. Illustrated by Remy Charlip.

——. *The Three Little Animals.* Harper, 1956. Illustrated by Garth Williams.

Brunhoff, Jean de, author-illustrator. *The Story of Babar, the Little Elephant.* Random, 1933.

Budney, Blossom. *A Kiss Is Round.* Lothrop, 1954. Illustrated by Vladimir Bobri.

Burningham, John, author-illustrator. *Harquin: The Fox Who Went Down to the Valley.* Bobbs, 1968.

——. *Mr. Gumpy's Outing.* Holt, 1971.

Burton, Virginia Lee, author-illustrator. *Katy and the Big Snow.* Houghton, 1943.

——. *The Little House.* Houghton, 1942.

Caldecott, Randolph, illustrator. See *The Frog He Would A-Wooing Go; The House That Jack Built.*

Cameron, Polly, author-illustrator. *I Can't, Said the Ant.* Coward, 1961.

Carigiet, Alois, author-illustrator. *The Pear Tree, the Birch Tree, and the Barberry Bush.* Walck, 1967.

Charlip, Remy, illustrator. *See* Brown, Margaret Wise, *The Dead Bird;* Miles, Betty.

Chaucer, Geoffrey. *Chanticleer and the Fox.* Crowell, 1958. Illustrated by Barbara Cooney.

Chermayeff, Ivan, illustrator. *See* Ott, John and Coley, Peter.

Cooney, Barbara, illustrator. *See* Chaucer, Geoffrey.

Cox, Palmer, author-illustrator. *The Brownies, Their Book.* Century, 1887.

Crane, Walter. See *Sing a Song of Sixpence.*

Cruse, Laurence. *See* Laurence.

Daugherty, James, author-illustrator. *Andy and the Lion.* Viking, 1938.

De Regniers, Beatrice. *Cats, Cats, Cats, Cats, Cats.* Pantheon, 1958. Illustrated by Bill Sokol.

——. *A Child's Book of Dreams.* Harcourt, 1957. Illustrated by Bill Sokol.

——. *A Little House of Your Own.* Harcourt, 1955. Illustrated by Irene Haas.

——. *The Snow Party.* Pantheon, 1959. Illustrated by Reiner Zimnik.

Diska, Pat. *Andy Says . . . Bonjour!* Vanguard, 1954. Illustrated by Chris Jenkyns.

Duvoisin, Roger, author-illustrator. *Veronica.* Knopf, 1961.

——, illustrator. *See* Fatio, Louise.

Eichenberg, Fritz, author-illustrator. *Ape in a Cape*. Harcourt, 1952.
——. *Dancing in the Moon*. Harcourt, 1956.
Emberley, Ed, author-illustrator. *A Wing on a Flea*. Little, 1961.
Fatio, Louise. *The Happy Lion*. McGraw, 1954. Illustrated by Roger Duvoisin.
Fischer, Hans, author-illustrator. *The Birthday*. Harcourt, 1954.
——. *Pitschi*. Harcourt, 1953.
——, illustrator. *See* Grimm, Jacob and Grimm, Wilhelm, *The Traveling Musicians*; Perrault, Charles, *Puss-in-Boots*.
Flack, Marjorie. *The Story About Ping*. Viking, 1933. Illustrated by Kurt Wiese.
Flora, James, author-illustrator. *Sherwood Walks Home*. Harcourt, 1966.
Fontane, Theodor. *Sir Ribbeck of Ribbeck of Havelland*. Macmillan, 1969. Illustrated by Nonny Hogrogian.
Foreman, Michael, author-illustrator. *The Two Giants*. Pantheon, 1967.
Francis, J. G., author-illustrator. *A Book of Cheerful Cats and Other Animated Animals*. Century, 1892.
François, André, illustrator. *See* Harris, Isobel; Stéphane, Nelly.
Françoise (pseud. for Françoise Seignobosc), author-illustrator. *Jeanne-Marie Counts Her Sheep*. Scribner's, 1951.
Frasconi, Antonio, author-illustrator. *See and Say*. Harcourt, 1955.
——. *The Snow and the Sun*. Harcourt, 1961.
——, illustrator. *See The House That Jack Built*.
Freeman, Don, author-illustrator. *Norman the Doorman*. Viking, 1959.
The Frog He Would A-Wooing Go. Warne, 1883. Illustrated by Randolph Caldecott.
Gachet, Jacqueline, author-illustrator. *The Ladybug*. McCall, 1970.
Gág, Wanda, author-illustrator. *Millions of Cats*. Coward, 1928.
Galdone, Paul, author-illustrator. *The Old Woman and Her Pig*. McGraw, 1960.
——, illustrator. *See* Titus, Eve.
Geisel, Theodor. *See* Seuss, Dr.
Goodall, John S., author-illustrator. *The Adventures of Paddy Pork*. Harcourt, 1968.
Graham, Margaret Bloy. *See* Zion, Gene.
Greenaway, Kate, author-illustrator. *Under the Window*. Warne, 1878.
Grimm, Jacob and Grimm, Wilhelm. *Rapunzel*. Harcourt, 1961. Illustrated by Felix Hoffmann.
——. *The Shoemaker and the Elves*. Scribner's, 1960. Illustrated by Adrienne Adams.
——. *Snow White and Rose Red*. Scribner's, 1964. Illustrated by Adrienne Adams.
——. *The Traveling Musicians*. Harcourt, 1955. Illustrated by Hans Fischer.

Haas, Irene, illustrator. *See* de Regniers, Beatrice, *A Little House of Your Own*.
Harper, Wilhelmina. *The Gunniwolf*. Dutton, 1967. Illustrated by William Wiesner.
Harris, Isobel. *Little Boy Brown*. Lippincott, 1949. Illustrated by André François.
Hewett, Anita. *The Little White Hen*. McGraw, 1963. Illustrated by William Stobbs.
Hoffmann, Felix, illustrator. *See* Grimm, Jacob and Grimm, Wilhelm, *Rapunzel*.
Hogrogian, Nonny, illustrator. *See* Fontane, Theodor.
The House That Jack Built. Warne, 1878. Illustrated by Randolph Caldecott.
——. Harcourt, 1958. Illustrated by Antonio Frasconi.
Huber, Ursula. *The Nock Family Circus*. Atheneum, 1968. Illustrated by Celestino Piatti.
Hughes, Shirley, author-illustrator. *Lucy and Tom's Day*. Scott, 1960.
Jenkyns, Chris, illustrator. *See* Diska, Pat.
Joslin, Sesyle. *What Do You Say, Dear?* Scott, 1958. Illustrated by Maurice Sendak.
Jüchen, Aurel von. *The Holy Night*. Atheneum, 1968. Illustrated by Celestino Piatti.
Kahl, Virginia, author-illustrator. *Away Went Wolfgang*. Scribner's 1954.
——. *The Duchess Bakes a Cake*. Scribner's, 1955.
Kepes, Juliet, author-illustrator. *Beasts from a Brush*. Pantheon, 1955.
——. *Lady Bird, Quickly*. Little, 1964.
——. *Two Little Birds and Three*. Houghton, 1960.
Klein, Leonore. *Henri's Walk to Paris*. Scott, 1962. Illustrated by Saul Bass.
Krauss, Ruth. *The Good Man and His Good Wife*. Harper, 1962. Illustrated by Marc Simont.
Kuskin, Karla, author-illustrator. *James and the Rain*. Harper, 1957.
La Fontaine, Jean de. *The Lion and the Rat*. Watts, 1963. Illustrated by Brian Wildsmith.
Laurence (pseud. of Laurence Cruse), author-illustrator. *A Village in Normandy*. Bobbs, 1968.
Lawrence, Jacob, author-illustrator. *Harriet and the Promised Land*. Simon, 1968.
Lawson, Robert, illustrator. *See* Leaf, Munro.
Leaf, Munro. *The Story of Ferdinand*. Viking, 1936. Illustrated by Robert Lawson.
Lent, Blair, illustrator. *See* Mosel, Arlene.
Lionni, Leo, author-illustrator. *Alexander and the Wind-Up Mouse*. Pantheon, 1969.
——. *Frederick*. Pantheon, 1967.
——. *Inch by Inch*. Obolensky, 1960.

126

———. *Little Blue and Little Yellow.* Obolensky, 1959.

———. *Swimmy.* Pantheon, 1963.

———. *Tico and the Golden Wings.* Pantheon, 1964.

Lipkind, William. *Finders Keepers.* Harcourt, 1951. Illustrated by Nicholas Mordvinoff.

———. *The Little Tiny Rooster.* Harcourt, 1960. Illustrated by Nicholas Mordvinoff.

———. *The Two Reds.* Harcourt, 1950. Illustrated by Nicholas Mordvinoff.

Lobel, Arnold, author-illustrator. *A Zoo for Mister Muster.* Harper, 1962.

Low, Joseph, author-illustrator. *Adam's Book of Odd Creatures.* Atheneum, 1962.

———. *Smiling Duke.* Houghton, 1963.

McCloskey, Robert, author-illustrator. *Blueberries for Sal.* Viking, 1948.

———. *Burt Dow, Deep-Water Man.* Viking, 1963.

———. *Make Way for Ducklings.* Viking, 1941.

McGinley, Phyllis. *Lucy McLockett.* Lippincott, 1959. Illustrated by Helen Stone.

Maley, Anne. *Have You Seen My Mother?* Carol Rhoda Books, Inc., 241 First Ave. N., Minneapolis, Minn. 55401, 1969. Illustrated by Yataka Sugita.

Miles, Betty. *A Day of Summer.* Knopf, 1960. Illustrated by Remy Charlip.

———. *A Day of Winter.* Knopf, 1961. Illustrated by Remy Charlip.

Mordvinoff, Nicholas, illustrator. *See* Lipkind, William.

Mosel, Arlene. *Tikki Tikki Tembo.* Holt, 1968. Illustrated by Blair Lent.

Munari, Bruno, author-illustrator. *Bruno Munari's ABC.* World, 1960.

Ness, Evaline, illustrator. *See* Nic Leodhas, Sorche.

Newberry, Clare Turlay, author-illustrator. *Pandora.* Harper, 1944.

Nicholson, William, author-illustrator. *An Alphabet.* Heinemann, 1898.

Nic Leodhas, Sorche. *All in the Morning Early.* Holt, 1963. Illustrated by Evaline Ness.

Otsuka, Yuzo. *Suho and the White Horse.* Bobbs, 1969. Illustrated by Suekichi Akaba.

Ott, John and Coley, Peter. *Peter Pumpkin.* Doubleday, 1963. Illustrated by Ivan Chermayeff.

Parker, Robert Andrew, illustrator. *See* Preston, Edna Mitchell.

Parkin, Rex, author-illustrator. *The Red Carpet.* Macmillan, 1948.

Peet, Bill, author-illustrator. *Hubert's Hair-Raising Adventure.* Houghton, 1959.

Perrault, Charles. *Cinderella.* Scribner's, 1954. Illustrated by Marcia Brown.

———. *Puss-in-Boots.* Scribner's, 1952. Illustrated by Marcia Brown.

———. *Puss-in-Boots.* Harcourt, 1959. Illustrated by Hans Fischer.

Peter Piper's Alphabet. Scribner's, 1959. Illustrated by Marcia Brown.

Piatti, Celestino, author-illustrator. *Celestino Piatti's Animal ABC.* Atheneum, 1966.

———. *The Happy Owls.* Atheneum, 1964.

———, illustrator. *See* Huber, Ursula; Jüchen, Aurel von.

Portal, Colette, illustrator. *See* Russell, Franklin.

Potter, Beatrix, author-illustrator. *The Tailor of Gloucester.* Warne, 1903.

———. *The Tale of Mrs. Tittlemouse.* Warne, 1910.

———. *The Tale of Peter Rabbit.* Warne, 1902.

Preston, Edna Mitchell. *Pop Corn and Ma Goodness.* Viking, 1969. Illustrated by Robert Andrew Parker.

Rand, Ann. *I Know a Lot of Things.* Harcourt, 1956. Illustrated by Paul Rand.

———. *So Small.* Harcourt, 1962. Illustrated by Feodor Rojankovsky.

———. *Sparkle and Spin.* Harcourt, 1957. Illustrated by Paul Rand.

Rand, Paul, illustrator. *See* Rand, Ann, *I Know a Lot of Things;* Rand, Ann, *Sparkle and Spin.*

Ransome, Arthur. *The Fool of the World and the Flying Ship.* Farrar, 1968. Illustrated by Uri Shulevitz.

Ray, Deborah, illustrator. *See* Welber, Robert.

Rey, Hans A. and Rey, Margaret. *Curious George.* Houghton, 1941. Illustrated by Hans A. Rey.

Richter, Marianne, illustrator. *See* Ruck-Pauquet, Gina.

Robbins, Ruth. *Baboushka and the Three Kings.* Parnassus, 1960. Illustrated by Nicolas Sidjakov.

Rojankovsky, Feodor, author-illustrator. *Animals in the Zoo.* Knopf, 1962.

———, illustrator. *See* Rand, Ann, *So Small.*

Ruck-Pauquet, Gina. *The Little Hedgehog.* Hastings, 1959. Illustrated by Marianne Richter.

Russell, Franklin. *The Honeybees.* Knopf, 1967. Illustrated by Colette Portal.

Schreiber, Georges, author-illustrator. *Bambino the Clown.* Viking, 1947.

Schmid, Eleonore, illustrator. *See* Baumann, Hans.

Seignobosc, Françoise. *See* Françoise.

Sendak, Maurice, author-illustrator. *Alligators All Around* (in "The Nutshell Library"). Harper, 1962.

———. *Pierre, a Cautionary Tale* (in "The Nutshell Library"). Harper, 1962.

———. *Where the Wild Things Are.* Harper, 1963.

———, illustrator. *See* Udry, Janice; Zolotow, Charlotte.

Seuss, Dr. (pseud. for Theodor Geisel), author-illustrator. *The 500 Hats of Bartholomew Cubbins.* Vanguard, 1938.

———. *Horton Hears a Who.* Random, 1954.

———. *If I Ran the Circus.* Random, 1956.

———. *The Sneetches and Other Stories.* Random, 1961.

———. *Thidwick, the Big-hearted Moose.* Random, 1948.

Shulevitz, Uri, illustrator. *See* Ransome, Arthur.

Sidjakov, Nicolas, illustrator. *See* Baker, Laura Nelson; Robbins, Ruth.

Simont, Marc, illustrator. *See* Krauss, Ruth.

Sing a Song of Sixpence. Warne, 1866. Illustrated by Walter Crane.

Singer, Isaac Bashevis. *Mazel and Shlimazel; or The Milk of a Lioness.* Farrar, 1967. Illustrated by Margot Zemach.

Smith, E. Boyd, author-illustrator. *The Chicken World.* Putnam, 1910.

Sokol, Bill, illustrator. *See* Andersen, Hans Christian, *The Emperor and the Nightingale;* de Regniers, Beatrice, *Cats, Cats, Cats, Cats, Cats;* de Regniers, Beatrice, *A Child's Book of Dreams.*

Stéphane, Nelly. *Roland.* Harcourt, 1958. Illustrated by André François.

Stobbs, William, illustrator. *See* Hewett, Anita.

Stone, Helen, illustrator. *See* McGinley, Phyllis.

Sugita, Yataka. *See* Maley, Anne.

Titus, Eve. *Anatole and the Cat.* McGraw, 1957. Illustrated by Paul Galdone.

Udry, Janice. *The Moon Jumpers.* Harper, 1959. Illustrated by Maurice Sendak.

Ungerer, Tomi, author-illustrator. *The Mellops' Go Spelunking.* Harper, 1963.

———. *Rufus.* Harper, 1961.

———. *Snail, Where Are You?* Harper, 1962.

Waber, Bernard, author-illustrator. *A Firefly Named Torchy.* Houghton, 1970.

———. *Rich Cat, Poor Cat.* Houghton, 1963.

Ward, Lynd, author-illustrator. *The Biggest Bear.* Houghton, 1952.

Weise, Kurt, illustrator. *See* Flack, Marjorie.

Welber, Robert. *Frog, Frog, Frog.* Pantheon, 1971. Illustrated by Deborah Ray.

———. *The Winter Picnic.* Pantheon, 1970. Illustrated by Deborah Ray.

Wildsmith, Brian, author-illustrator. *Brian Wildsmith's ABC.* Watts, 1963.

———. *Brian Wildsmith's Birds.* Watts, 1967.

———, illustrator. *See* La Fontaine, Jean de.

Williams, Garth, illustrator. *See* Brown, Margaret Wise, *The Three Little Animals.*

Wondriska, William, author-illustrator. *The Tomato Patch.* Holt, 1964.

———. *Which Way to the Zoo?* Holt, 1962.

Wyndham, Robert. *Chinese Mother Goose Rhymes.* World, 1968. Illustrated by Ed Young.

Yashima, Taro, author-illustrator. *The Seashore Story.* Viking, 1967.

———. *Umbrella.* Viking, 1958.

———. *The Village Tree.* Viking, 1953.

Young, Ed, illustrator. *See* Wyndham, Robert.

Zemach, Harve. *The Judge; An Untrue Tale.* Farrar, 1969. Illustrated by Margot Zemach.

———. *Nail Soup.* Follett, 1964. Illustrated by Margot Zemach.

———, ed. *Mommy, Buy Me a China Doll.* Follett, 1966. Illustrated by Margot Zemach.

Zemach, Margot, illustrator. *See* Singer, Isaac Bashevis; Zemach, Harve.

Zimnik, Reiner, author-illustrator. *The Bear on the Motorcycle.* Atheneum, 1963.

———. *Jonah the Fisherman.* Pantheon, 1956.

———, illustrator. *See* de Regniers, Beatrice, *The Snow Party.*

Zion, Gene. *Harry the Dirty Dog.* Harper, 1956. Illustrated by Margaret Bloy Graham.

———. *No Roses for Harry.* Harper, 1958. Illustrated by Margaret Bloy Graham.

Zolotow, Charlotte. *Mr. Rabbit and the Lovely Present.* Harper, 1962. Illustrated by Maurice Sendak.

References

Introduction: The Diminutive Bookman

1. Peter and Iona Opie, *The Lore and Language of Schoolchildren* (London: Oxford University Press, 1959), pp. 12, 18, 20.
2. Federico García Lorca, *Three Tragedies* (New York: New Directions, 1956), p. 5.
3. Jacques Barzun, *The Energies of Art* (New York: Vintage Books, 1962), p. 7.
4. Lillian Smith, *The Unreluctant Years: A Critical Approach to Children's Literature* (Chicago: American Library Association, 1953).
5. Ludwig Bemelmans, "Caldecott Award Acceptance," *Horn Book Magazine*, XXX (August 1954), 271.

1 Historical Perspective

1. David Bland, *The Illustration of Books* (New York: Pantheon, 1952), p. 40.
2. *Ibid.*, p. 83.
3. *Ibid.*, pp. 99–100.
4. David Bland, *A History of Book Illustration: The Illuminated Manuscript & the Printed Book*, rev. ed. (Berkeley: University of California Press, 1969), p. 224.
5. *Ibid.*, p. 223.
6. Bettina Hürlimann, *Three Centuries of Children's Books in Europe* (New York: World, 1968), p. 57.
7. David Bland, *A History of Book Illustration*, p. 268.
8. Paul G. Konody, *The Art of Walter Crane* (London: George Bell & Sons, 1902), p. 27.
9. Janet Adam Smith, *Children's Illustrated Books* (London: Collins, 1949), p. 9.
10. Bertha E. Mahony and others, "*Illustrators of Children's Books, 1744–1945,*" (Boston: Horn Book, 1947), p. 71.
11. Philip James, *English Book Illustration, 1800–1900* (London: King Penguin Books, 1947), p. 63.
12. David Bland, *A History of Book Illustration*, p. 388.
13. Jacques Barzun, *The Energies of Art* (New York: Vintage Books, 1962), p. vii.

2 Stereotypes in Illustration

1. "The Child and the Artist," *Times Literary Supplement* (London), November 23, 1933, p. 803.
2. Nicholas Mordvinoff, "Caldecott Award Acceptance," *Horn Book Magazine*, XXVIII (August 1952), p. 222.
3. Ben Shahn, *The Shape of Content* (New York: Vintage Books, 1957), p. 124.

3 Graphic Elements

1. Leo Steinberg, "The Eye Is Part of the Mind," in *Reflections on Art; A Source Book of Writings by Artists, Critics, and Philosophers*, ed. Susanne K. Langer (New York: Oxford University Press, 1961), p. 247.

2. Ben Shahn, *The Shape of Content* (New York: Vintage Books, 1957), p. 57.
3. Selden Rodman, *Conversations with Artists* (New York: Capricorn Books, 1961), p. 218.
4. *Ibid.*, p. 173.
5. *Ibid.*, p. 109.
6. Vincent van Gogh, *Letters* (Cassirer Publications, 1914), p. 16.

5 Book Design

1. David Bland, *The Illustration of Books* (New York: Pantheon, 1952), p. 13.
2. *Ibid.*, p. 14.
3. Marcia Brown, "My Goals as an Illustrator," *Horn Book Magazine*, XLIII (June 1967), 310.
4. Jean Poindexter Colby, *The Children's Book Field* (New York: Pellegrini and Cudahy, 1952), p. 138.

6 Literary Elements

1. C. S. Lewis, *An Experiment in Criticism* (London: Cambridge University Press, 1961), pp. 21–22.
2. Frances Clarke Sayers, *Summoned by Books*, comp. Marjeanne Jensen Blinn (New York: Viking, 1965), p. 61.
3. Lewis, *op. cit.*, p. 140.
4. Elizabeth Bowen, "Rx for a Story Worth the Telling," *New York Times Book Review*, August 31, 1958, p. 1.
5. P. M. Pickard, *I Could a Tale Unfold; Violence, Horror, and Sensationalism in Stories for Children* (New York: Humanities Press, 1961), p. 50.
6. Frank L. Lucas, *Style* (New York: Collier Books, 1962), p. 7.
7. John Greenway, *Literature Among the Primitives* (Detroit: Folklore Associates, 1964).
8. Rumer Godden, "Words Make the Book," *Writer*, LXXVII (July 1964), 16.
9. *Ibid.*, p. 17.
10. Rumer Godden, *Hans Christian Andersen: A Great Life in Brief* (New York: Knopf, 1955), p. 146.
11. Georg Brandes, *Creative Spirits of the Nineteenth Century* (New York: Crowell, 1923), p. 3.
12. I. A. Richards, *Principles of Literary Criticism* (New York: Harcourt, 1925), pp. 134–135.
13. Dorothy M. White (Neal), *About Books for Children* (London: Oxford University Press, 1958), p. 44.

7 Outstanding Narrative Writers

1. Robert Cahn, "The Wonderful World of Dr. Seuss," *Saturday Evening Post*, CCXXX (July 6, 1957), 46.
2. *Ibid.*
3. *Ibid.*
4. Meryle Secrest, "No Such Thing as a Child's Book," *Des Moines Register*, December 12, 1970, p. 16.
5. Carolyn Horovitz, "Fiction and the Paradox of Play," *Wilson Library Bulletin*, XLIV (December 1969), 397–398.
6. Nat Hentoff, "Among the Wild Things," in *Only Connect: Readings on Children's Literature*, ed. Sheila Egoff and others (New York: Oxford University Press, 1969), p. 343.
7. Jacques Barchilon and Henry Pettit, *The Authentic Mother Goose Fairy Tales and Nursery Rhymes* (Denver: Alan Swallow, 1960), p. 27.

8. Bettina Hürlimann, *Three Centuries of Children's Books in Europe* (New York: World, 1968), p. 198.

9. *Ibid.*, p. 196.

10. Jane Holtz Kay, "Curious George Lives Here," *Christian Science Monitor* (Boston), May 9, 1970, p. 15.

11. *Ibid.*

12. Jean Karl, *From Childhood to Childhood; Children's Books and Their Creators* (New York: John Day, 1970), p. 81.

13. Geoffrey Trease, *Tales Out of School: A Survey of Children's Fiction* (London: Heinemann, 1949), p. 57.

8 Specialized Texts

1. F. J. Harvey Darton, *Children's Books in England; Five Centuries of Social Life*, 2 ed. (London: Cambridge University Press, 1960), p. 48.

2. *Peter Piper's Practical Principles of Plain and Perfect Pronunciation* (New York: Dover, 1970), from the "Prefatory Note."

9 The Caldecott Award

1. Irene Smith, *A History of the Newbery and Caldecott Medals* (New York: Viking, 1957), p. 103.

2. *Ibid.*, p. 65.

3. *Ibid.*, p. 103.

4. *Ibid.*, p. 72.

5. *Ibid.*, p. 100.

6. *Ibid.*, p. 79.

7. *Ibid.*, p. 66.

8. *Ibid.*, p. 64.

9. Robert Cahn, "The Wonderful World of Dr. Seuss," *Saturday Evening Post*, CCXXX (July 6, 1957), 46.

10. Nicholas Mordvinoff, "Caldecott Award Acceptance," *Horn Book Magazine*, XXVIII (August 1952), 222.

10 The Child, the Librarian, and the Critic

1. Margot Hentoff, "Little Private Lives," *New York Review of Books*, XV (December 17, 1970), 10.

2. *Ibid.*

3. James Higgins, *Beyond Words: Mystical Fancy in Children's Literature* (New York: Teachers College Press, 1970), p. 50.

4. Clive Bell, *Art* (New York: Capricorn Books, 1958), p. 62.

5. Hentoff, *loc. cit.*

6. Henry James, "The Art of Fiction," in *Makers of Literary Criticism*, comp., ed. A. G. George (London: Asia Publishing House, 1968), Vol. 2, p. 352.

7. Nicolas Sidjakov, "Caldecott Award Acceptance," *Horn Book Magazine*, XXXVII (August 1961), 320.

8. Henry Seidel Canby, *Definitions: Essays in Contemporary Criticism; Second Series* (Port Washington, N.Y.: Kennikat Press, 1967), p. 218.

9. Ludwig Bemelmans, "Caldecott Award Acceptance," *Horn Book Magazine*, XXX (August 1954), 271.

Index

References to reproductions of illustrations are printed in boldface type.